Man and Woman:
A Divine Invention

Man and Woman:
A Divine Invention

ALICE VON HILDEBRAND
with the assistance of Henry Russell

Foreword by Benedict J. Groeschel, C.F.R.

Sapientia Press
of Ave Maria University

Copyright © 2010 by Alice von Hildebrand. All rights reserved.

No part of this publication may be reproduced or transmitted in any form or means, electronic or mechanical, including photography, recording, or any other information storage or retrieval system, without permission in writing from the publisher.

Requests for permission to make copies of any part of the work should be directed to:

Sapientia Press
of Ave Maria University
5050 Ave Maria Blvd.
Ave Maria, FL 34142
888-343-8607

Cover Images

Detail from Hans Memling (1425/40–1494), *Tommaso di Folco Portinari* (1428–1501). Probably 1470. Overall $17\,3/8 \times 13\,1/4$ in. (44.1 x 33.7 cm), painted surface $16\,5/8 \times 12\,1/2$ in. (42.2 x 31.8 cm). Pendant to the portrait of Maria Portinari. The Metropolitan Museum of Art, Bequest of Benjamin Altman, 1913 (14.40.626). Photo Credit: Image copyright © The Metropolitan Museum of Art/Source: Art Resource, New York.

Detail from Hans Memling (1425/40–1494), *Maria Portinari* (Maria Maddalena Baroncelli, born 1456). Probably 1470. Overall $17\,3/8 \times 13\,3/8$ in. (44.1 x 34 cm); painted surface $16\,5/8 \times 12\,5/8$ in. (42.2 x 32.1 cm). Pendant to the portrait of Tommaso Portinari. The Metropolitan Museum of Art, Bequest of Benjamin Altman, 1913 (14.40.627). Photo Credit: Image copyright © The Metropolitan Museum of Art/Source: Art Resource, New York.

Cover Design

Eloise Anagnost

Printed in the United States of America.

Library of Congress Control Number: 2009943667

ISBN: 978-1-932589-56-6

*Dedicated to His Excellency,
Raymond Archbishop Burke,
with profound admiration and gratitude.*

Contents

Foreword ix
Acknowledgments................................. xi
Introduction xiii

CHAPTER 1
"In the Beginning..." 1
   Original Sin: The Tragic Separation 5
   Consequences of Brokenness 7
   Distortion of the Male Genius: The Brute 11
   Distortion of the Female Genius:
   The Seductress..................................... 13
   A Caution on Generalizations...................... 16

CHAPTER 2
The Terrible Lie of Feminism 19
   Some Contemporary Thinkers
   on Feminism 20
   The War on Femininity............................. 26
   The War on Poetry and Beauty..................... 34
   The War on Spiritual Ecology 37
   Supernatural Blindness:
   Triumphant Secularism 39

Conclusion 40

CHAPTER 3
The Feminine Genius: Mystery, Veiling, Piety, and Modesty 41

    Fecundity 47

    Receptivity 57

    Frailty, Thy Name Is Woman 59

        The Liturgy and the Saints
in Praise of Womanhood 59

        The Gift of Weakness:
Humility as Teacher 64

    The Moral Fiber of Women 71

CHAPTER 4
With Mary: From Defeat to Victory 77

    Mary as Exemplar: *Stella Matutina*
(The Morning Star) 77

    Mother Most Pure 80

    Ark of the Covenant: Gate of Heaven 86

    Singular Vessel of Devotion: Reverence 89

    Virgin Most Faithful: Piety 91

    Seat of Wisdom: Refutation of All Heresies 93

    Comfort of the Afflicted: *Mater Dolorosa* 95

CHAPTER 5
*Women and Relationship:
Women and Motherhood* 99

    Virginity: The Perfect Form
of Motherhood 105

    Saintly Family Relationships 108

        Holy Spouses 108

Mothers and Sons 111
  Saint Augustine............................ 111
  Other Saints............................... 113
Fathers and Daughters 114
  Saint Thomas More 114
  Saint Teresa of Avila....................... 119
  Saint Thérèse of Lisieux.................... 122
Holy Siblings 123
Holy Friendships 126

CHAPTER 6
Women and the Priesthood 139
Holy Discrimination.............................. 140
Holy Discrimination Versus
Dictatorial Relativism 142
Non Serviam 147
The Obedience of the Creature................... 151
Defiance Masquerading as Doubt................ 154
The Distorted Question of Feminine
Priesthood: No Entitlement...................... 156
Maternity and the Priesthood 163
Maternal Aspirations 165
Modest Appearance 167
A Vocation of Obedience 169
Arguments Fall on Deaf Ears 172
Saint Thérèse of Lisieux
and the Priesthood................................ 175

Foreword

As one has come to expect of Dr. Alice von Hildebrand, this book is a clear philosophical and theological statement of the relationship between men and women. Dr. von Hildebrand has wisely avoided the host of constantly competing opinions and ideas that are so frequently presented to us as truth concerning this important topic. These theories for too many years shaped our ideas of reality concerning sexuality. She is not interested in ideas about truth that change with the times. Instead, she is concerned with eternal truth, and she understands quite well that the relationship between man and woman—a relationship she rightly calls a "divine invention"—finds its meaning in the eternal truth of God's plan for us. As Winston Churchill once said, "[The] truth is incontrovertible. Panic may resent it, ignorance may deride it, malice may distort it, but there it is."¹ These are words that Dr. von Hildebrand could have said herself.

This book will be invaluable and refreshing to those who have put up for too long with a great deal of confusion regarding the relationship of men and women and especially regarding the real purpose and importance of human sexuality. These problems and misunderstandings can be found wherever we look, even in religious circles, and a book such as this one is exactly what we need to counteract them. As always, Dr. von Hildebrand is clear and concise. Her wide-ranging understanding of Western thought is obvious in this book, as is the fact that throughout much of history, our great thinkers and writers have far more often been in basic agreement with the Catholic Church's understanding of sexuality than with the ideas that are currently in vogue. *Man and Woman: A Divine Invention* is a short but bracing statement of reality, made during a time when reality has become indistinguishable from opinion. It will be a major help in restoring sanity and holiness to an area that has too long been chaotic. This is a book that offers us insights that are not only philosophical and theological but spiritual as well.

—FR. BENEDICT GROESCHEL, C.F.R.

---

[1] *Churchill by Himself: The Definitive Collection of Quotations*, ed. Richard Langworth (London: Ebury Press; New York: Public Affairs, 2008), 27.

Acknowledgments

Those of us dealing with publishers are bound to raise the question, what are the qualifications a true editor should possess? May I suggest that it is someone who is so perceptive that he intuits an author's intentions even though they are clumsily formulated. He reverently and intelligently reads the text, and while inserting no opinions of his own, truly fulfills the author's intentions. This is why my debt to Henry Russell is a very great one. Lucky are the authors whose work is confided to him.

Another person who has been crucial in easing "labor pains" is my friend Diane Eriksen. I have dealt with many managing editors in my life, but working with her has been so pleasing that it could tempt me to write another book, something unwise at my age.

I also wish to mention my very dear god-child Stephanie Block, at one point my student and now my friend, whose loving dedication in reading my manuscript deserves a special commendation.

Introduction

Pascal wrote that "man is the most amazing object in nature."[1] Indeed, we are such complex beings that not only do we have great difficulties understanding others, but worse, we have great difficulties understanding ourselves.

For reasons that we need not investigate, the Creator chose to create beings that are doubly complex; for not only did He make man to be comprised of soul and body—a spiritual reality and a material one—but moreover, to crown this complexity, "male and female he created them."[2] Clearly, the fullness of human nature is to be found in the perfect union between man and woman, who have both a body and a soul.

This is indeed "a divine invention" that would never have entered man's head. It is so simple to be

---

[1] "L'homme est à lui-même le plus prodigieux object de la nature." Blaise Pascal, *Pensées* (Paris: Ant. Aug. Renouard, 1812), pt. 1, art. 6, no. 26, p. 215.

[2] Gen 1:27.

"just a chimpanzee," or "just an angel," but to be essentially made up of two very different realities—both of which are meant to be related to another person—sheds light on our difficulty to understand others and to understand ourselves.

In Eden, God had created perfect harmony between the body and the soul, and between Adam and Eve. In God's plans, the body benefited the soul, and the soul benefited the body; the body qua body is not a person. But through its union with an immortal soul, man's body was personified; that is, it was "knighted." Physical organs were given both dignity and symbolic meaning. For instance, we can think of the role of the heart in the spiritual life, and the dignity of the female womb, which is the tabernacle of a new life.

But through original sin—a metaphysical revolt against God—this harmony was badly disrupted. From that moment on, man has been born on a battlefield. He must fight on two fronts: First, with God's help, he is called upon to reharmonize his body and his soul, for the former—imitating man's revolt against God—no longer obeys the directives given by the soul; it claims its own independence. Second, man is called upon to span the chasm that has disrupted the union of Adam and Eve.

Let us first turn to the revolt of the flesh against the spirit. In Paradise, our first parents found themselves in a garden of beauty rich in enjoyments. All of these delights, whether physical, psychological, or spiritual, were gratefully accepted as coming from the Giver of all gifts.

The very moment that man turned against God, the body started making demands upon the soul, one of them being the craving for pleasures, viewed no longer as gifts but as "rights."

Man, made in God's image and likeness, was now exposed to the temptation of following animal cravings, which put such pressure upon the soul that the soul often suffered defeat. The body, in its satisfaction of cravings, became arrogant, often leaving the soul no peace until these desires were fulfilled. Man's instincts waged war on man's spiritual nature, trying—to quote Plato—"to nail the soul to the body."[3]

Not only did these cravings, when fulfilled, lead to other cravings, but when not granted, they usually triggered rage. Babies are not the only ones who go into tantrums when their wishes are not satisfied. These rages can be so violent that the soul—exhausted—gives in to have peace. How profound were the words of Plato that one of the

---

[3] "Every pleasure and pain has, as one may say, a nail, with which it nails and buckles her [the soul] to the body and gives her a bodily shape, fancying anything to be true which the body on its part asserts to be so." *Plato's Phædo*, trans. E. M. Cope (Cambridge: Cambridge University Press, 1875), no. 83, p. 50.

main aims of education should be to train a child to achieve "victory over pleasure."[4]

Not only did legitimate pleasures clamor to be satisfied to the point of abuse (be it in food or drink), but alas, illegitimate pleasures joined forces with them. Evil generates evil, and perverse pleasures invaded man's consciousness; they are legion. This explains why God regretted that He had created man.[5] Modern technology, unfortunately, can be in devilish hands. How many television channels eloquently invite man to diabolical actions, clearly aiming at staining God's image in the human soul?

Two conclusions can be drawn. First, since original sin, man has to fight to keep his freedom. He must daily oppose temptation coming from "below." No one has expressed this more eloquently than Saint Augustine in his *Confessions*: metaphysically, we are free; morally, we are often slaves.[6] To reconquer this freedom, we need to acknowledge that we are responsible for the chains that bind us and turn to God's grace for help. To humbly admit our guilt and turn to God for help is the way to change defeat into victory, as witnessed by the bishop of Hippo.

The second conclusion is that the union between body and soul is so close that, until the two harmo-

---

[4] Plato, *The Laws*, trans. Benjamin Jowett (New York: Cosimo, 2008), no. 840, p. 191.

[5] Gen 6:6.

[6] Augustine, *Confessions*, bk. 8, nos. 10ff.

nize according to the guidance of the Divine Conductor, it is sheer illusion to assume that the communion with the other sex—also disrupted by sin—can be accomplished. The more our bodies and our souls sing the same song, whose notes were written by the Creator, the better the chance that the two complementary sexes will create beautiful music. That this is possible is the theme of this book.

CHAPTER 1

"In the Beginning . . ."

"God created man in his own image . . . male and female he created them."[1] This is the luminous climax of the story of creation. God saw that "it was good."[2] Nature's beauty spoke eloquently of His glory, but its crown was the creation of a human person: a being who is not only a trace of God (*vestigium*, as Saint Bonaventure calls it)[3] but His image. Two key ideas stand out in the climax of the book of Genesis. First, the fullness of human nature is to be found in man *and* woman. This is truly a divine invention. Second, man is composed of both body and soul. Male and female, body and soul: the human person is, therefore, a double mystery. The plenitude of human nature is found only in the unity of male and female. *Homo* (man) is not to be found only in the male (*vir*), nor is it to be found only in the

---
[1] Gen 1:26.
[2] Gen 1:21.
[3] See, for example, Bonaventure, *The Soul's Journey into God*, chap. 2, nos. 1–7.

female (*mulier*). It is in both, together. They are two beings of equal dignity, but complementary; therefore, they are mutually necessary for enriching one another. Read in the light of the New Testament, these dual unities of creation foreshadow the mystery of mysteries: the Incarnation. A key concern of this book is to try to shed some modest light on this mystery, a light borrowed from the New Testament, which, fulfilling the Old Testament, has shown how holiness alone can unify a being of such complexity.

Adam was created first. Since a person is made for communion—just as the Holy Trinity is a perfect communion of Persons—God declared that it was not good for him to be alone. None of the animals was worthy to be Adam's companion. The most handsome and attractive chimpanzee was rejected as unworthy. The chasm between impersonal and personal beings is so profound[4] that "the missing link" is sought for in vain. Human beings alone have an immortal *soul* directly created by God; the soul cannot possibly be the fruit of "evolution." Man's body may be called a *factum* (a thing made, a fact). His soul is a *genitum* (something begotten, not made).

Eve, the first woman, was from the beginning given a special dignity because her body was formed, not from the dust of the earth, as Adam's

---

[4] Dietrich von Hildebrand, in *Metaphysik der Gemeinschaft*, calls it the greatest abyss after the one between Creator and creature.

was, but from another living person. When Adam woke from the deep sleep in which God had put him in order to form Eve's body, seeing her, he exclaimed with overwhelming joy: "This at last is bone of my bones and flesh of my flesh."[5] He proclaimed that finally he was meeting someone of equal ontological dignity. Although all animals were meant to be under man's dominion, Eve was his soul mate and ontologically equal to him. His response was enchantment.

Moses does not tell us of Eve's response upon perceiving the man who was to be her husband, but we can assume that it was awe and admiration for his nobility, his strength, his courage, and his masculinity. This is the classical response of every woman meeting a man who lives up to his calling. Eve knew intuitively that Adam complemented her and that they belonged together so closely that the plenitude of human nature was to be found in their union.

That God has created two creatures of equal dignity with different genders is truly divinely inspired. To borrow a sentence from Kierkegaard, "It would never have entered man's head."[6] Not

---

[5] Gen 2:23.

[6] "To be so near to God as Christianity teaches that man can come to Him, and dare come to Him, and shall come to Him in Christ, has never entered into any man's head." Søren Kierkegaard, *The Sickness unto Death*, trans. Walter Lowrie (Princeton, N.J.: Princeton University Press, 1941), p. 206.

only are man and woman made for each other, not only do they complement each other, but, above all, their differences (which are not limited to the biological sphere) enable them to be partners with God Himself in creating new human persons. This privilege was not granted to angels. It is a sacred partnership that signaled, from the very beginning, the mystery and depth of human engendering.

There are certainly reasons why angels could feel a "holy envy" toward human creatures: man's collaboration with God in procreating other humans, the reality that the second Person of the Holy Trinity became man, and the fact that the blessed one among women received the unheard-of privilege of changing the diapers of the God-man. That the most humble task can be a privilege highlights the fact that man's glorification of God is to be measured, not by the rank of task one is accomplishing, *but by the love with which it is performed*. Every single action of the Holy Virgin, however modest, glorified God more than any noble task performed by any of the saints, who inevitably loved God less. Even while sleeping, the blessed one was eloquently singing God's praise.

The beginning of Genesis eloquently sketches man's greatness. He is made in God's image and likeness and is made for communion; that is to say, love is meant to play a fundamental role in his life.

ORIGINAL SIN: THE TRAGIC SEPARATION

Then came the tragedy of original sin. All the dreadful consequences that follow in its train are well known: man is separated from God and cannot by himself span the abyss that sin has created. His noble nature is severely wounded. His intelligence is darkened, his will is weakened, and his heart is hardened. He will suffer and die. There is no sign of repentance in the culprits—Adam blames Eve, and Eve blames the serpent: a *Psychology Today* case of *tua culpa*.[7]

Our concern, however, is to shed light on another consequence, which, to our knowledge, is often omitted or improperly understood. *The greatest separation that can divide human persons takes place the very moment that they separate themselves from God by sin*. Sin separates sinners from one another. How profoundly significant that as soon as they sinned, Adam and Eve discovered that they were naked, felt shame, and hid themselves. Every crime brings about its own punishment.[8] From this moment on, the beautiful harmony that God established between Adam and Eve—their mutual enchantment and admiration, their fruitful complementarity—was ruptured. Their beauty was obscured.

---

[7] The Catholic Liturgy teaches man to acknowledge his own sinfulness, saying *mea culpa*—*my* fault. The response of fallen human nature is to blame someone else, saying *tua culpa*—*your* fault.

[8] Cf. Augustine, *Confessions*, bk. 1, no. 19.

The fact that Adam and Eve sinned *together* created a chasm between them that resonates throughout the ages to this very day. Daily experiences teach us that people who "shack up" together or follow the dictates of "free love," without a serious commitment taken in front of God, are bound to part, sooner or later. Even though they believe this "freedom" allows them to be closer together, it has quite the opposite effect. Statistics tell us that 40 percent of births in the United States come from single mothers.[9] How many of these were abandoned by boyfriends for "imprudent" failure to practice "safe sex," forgetting to "take the pill," or "irresponsibly" refusing an abortion?

The moment that a person's approach to the other sex is grounded in self-satisfaction, disassociated pleasure, or momentary excitement, he is tragically separated from the possibility of true love. The moment he acts without respect for a fellow creature of God (made in His image and likeness) and without respect for the divine law governing procreation, he and his partner in crime are bound—and this is a law that admits of no exception—to be tragically separated from one another. The closest physical bond that can exist between human beings, to "become one flesh,"[10] instead becomes the key agent of their separation.

---

[9] Associated Press, "Unwed birthrate reaches all-time high in U.S.," March 18, 2009, www.msnbc.msn.com/id/29754561/ns/health-womens_health (accessed April 6, 2009).

[10] Mk 10:8.

With the Fall, lust made its entrance into our fallen world and into the mysterious sphere in which God deigned to collaborate with man and woman to bring new human persons into the world. Human sexuality became a domain in which Satan particularly showed his diabolical power within wounded human nature. Most of his easy victories take place here. Fornication, adultery, incest, rape, and sexual perversions all take place in the preferred expression of Adam and Eve's oneness, in their becoming one flesh.

CONSEQUENCES OF BROKENNESS

The devastation wrought in the intimate sphere by original sin caused God to regret that He had created man, one of the saddest moments in the Bible.[11] Inspired by the devil, men have been particularly inventive in deviating from God's beautiful plan that created Adam and Eve "male and female."

The greatness of the Bible, and one of the marks by which we know it to be true, is that, far from hiding scandalous sins committed by towering figures, it relates their faults in detail. Even the Chosen People were affected. It is a source of grief to read that Judah slept with his daughter-in-law, believing her to be a prostitute. The great David was an adulterer and a murderer. Thanks to the prophet Nathan, David's eyes were opened to the abomination of his

---

[11] Gen 6:7.

crimes, and he repented—in one of the most beautiful and poignant of his psalms, the *Miserere* (Psalm 51). His son Amnon raped his half sister Tamar and, after having shamed her, nourished a fierce hatred (typically enough) of the woman whose life he had ruined. David was angry but did not punish him; he favored this son because "he was his first-born"![12] Later, Absalom revenged his sister by killing Amnon. These are certainly not uplifting stories.

The book of Tobit contains one of the most powerful texts in the Old Testament on the damage done to the intimate sphere by sin. Sarah, Raguel's daughter, had been married seven times; each one of her seven husbands was struck dead in the bridal chamber as soon as he approached her. But Tobias, instructed by the angel Raphael, whom he called Azariah, was informed of what he should do in order to prevent the evil one from killing him. Whereas the previous husbands were clearly animated by lust, Tobias turned to Sarah with the following words: "Sister, get up, and let us pray and implore our Lord that he grant us mercy and safety. . . . Now, O Lord, I am not taking this sister of mine because of lust, but with sincerity. Grant that I may find mercy and may grow old together with her."[13] How one wishes that every single couple preparing for marriage memorized these words.

---

[12] 2 Sam 13:21 (New American Bible [NAB]).
[13] Tob 8:4, 7.

Are they ever mentioned today in the instructions given to engaged couples? This passage shows both how the intimate sphere has been damaged by sin, since lust is the enemy of love, and simultaneously, how our wounds can be healed by prayer. It is the most eloquent portent in the Old Testament of the wondrous healing that Mary will bring in the New Testament by her charity and her obedience to God's will, both before and within the married state. Either God or Satan is in the bridal chamber.

Contemporary man has lost what Dante calls the "hope to gain the mountain top."[14] Today, many young people, even Catholics, are cynical and despair of ever achieving a happy marriage. They are convinced that most unions end in bitterness and disaster; they "console" themselves with exciting, short-lived affairs that, perhaps, give short-term pleasure. The hope of achieving true happiness is abandoned. This is strikingly expressed in the words of the French poet Paul Valéry: "God created man and finding him not sufficiently alone, gave him a female companion to make him feel his solitude more keenly."[15]

This aloneness is a refrain in several of Gabriel Marcel's theatrical pieces. One of his most poignant quotations is "There is only one suffering—to be

---

[14] *Dante's "The Inferno,"* trans. Anthony Esolen (New York: Modern Library, 2005), canto 1, line 54, p. 5.

[15] Paul Valéry, *A Book of French Quotations*, compiled by Norbert Guterman (New York: Doubleday, 1963), p. 383.

alone."[16] Another one of his characters exclaims, "It is fearful how lonesome I can feel at times."[17] Since man is made for communion, why is "loneliness" so epidemic?

As we have considered, sin creates a chasm between the guilty pairs, and this chasm—like the chasm between them and their Creator—is so deep that, by themselves, they are incapable of bridging it. The sexual sphere is particularly broken. Our Lady of Fatima intimated that the majority of sins are committed precisely in the human experience that was intended to express love, self-giving, and chastity. Where tenderness reigns, concupiscence recedes.[18] Where concupiscence reigns, artificial contraception and abortion inevitably follow.

There is, however, an alternative to despair. Not only may the sinner hope, but he also has the blessed guarantee, that terrible disappointments and wounds can be healed through the purity of Mary, the blessed Mother of God. He can benefit from the graces of redemption. He can avail himself of the help of a Savior born of Mary's perfect humanity.

---

[16] "Il n'y a qu'une souffrance, c'est d'être seul." Gabriel Marcel, *Le coeur des autres* (Paris: Bernard Grasset, 1921), act 3, scene 3, p. 111.

[17] Gabriel Marcel, *Vers un autre Royaume* (1963), p. 18.

[18] Dietrich von Hildebrand, *In Defense of Purity* (New York: Sheed and Ward, 1935), chap. 20.

DISTORTION OF THE MALE GENIUS: THE BRUTE

We have mentioned briefly some of the characteristics of Adam: nobility, strength, chivalry, and objectivity. Eve, too, was given typically female gems: gentleness, empathy, warmth, devotion, and mystery. Sin ravaged these noble traits. From the very moment that Adam and Eve sinned, their most notable virtues degenerated into caricatures. Brutality and cold-hearted objectivity threatened Adam's strength. All too often, he turned his God-given authority into an abuse of power for his own selfish aims by totally ignoring the fact *that to be given authority means to serve those who are confided to the care of whomever is given such responsibility.*

Most tragically, his noble male heart became a desert in which feelings, however noble, failed to blossom. How many men, deluded by a foolish *machismo*, view "feelings"—compassion, tenderness, or contrition—as being despicable signs of female weakness, that is, of effeminacy? For example, recall Nietzsche's contempt for pity, which he thought should be rejected by any "great soul," for he viewed pity as a weakness,[19] as hypocritical,[20] and as unworthy of noble men.[21]

---

[19] Friedrich Nietzsche, *Morgenröte*, in *Nietzsche-Register*, by Richard Oehler (Stuttgart: Alfred Kröner Verlag, 1965), p. 121.

[20] Friedrich Nietzsche, *Menschliches, Allzumenschliches*, vol. 2, in Oehler, *Nietzsche-Register*.

[21] Nietzsche, *Morgenröte*, ibid., p. 22.

Anyone acquainted with great literature has witnessed, time and again, how male virtues may deteriorate into horrible abuses. In his great work *The Possessed*, Dostoyevsky refers to the savage beatings that Lebyadkin inflicts, when drunk, upon his crippled sister Liza. Her response is a boundless contempt. When men are in a state of inebriety, the wild animal in them is let loose, and women are usually their preferred victims. Gogol's *Taras Bulba* gives us a similar scenario. Bulba's two sons come home after a long absence. Their mother's joy and the expression of her tenderness is viewed by him as a threat to their masculinity. Fully aware that he is breaking her heart, he shortens their visit to a few hours from fear that they would be "softened" and contaminated by her affectivity. His disdain of women is revolting. We find a similar depressing scenario in Chekhov's short story entitled "The Peasants." One of the characters, Kiriak, mercilessly beats his wife, Maria, as soon as he comes home. He is, of course, drunk. His intolerable conduct is regretted but not sharply condemned: "But despite all this, they were men, they suffered and wept as men; and in their whole lives there was not one act for which an excuse might not be found."[22] It goes unmentioned that such behavior demands contrition.

---

[22] Anton Chekhov, "The Peasants," in *The Works of Anton Chekhov* (New York: W. J. Black, 1929), p. 161.

With Teutonic brutality, Nietzsche writes, "When you go to a woman, don't forget your whip,"[23] and he quotes the Italian proverb "Buona e mala femmina vuol bastone" (whether good or bad, a woman should be beaten).[24] Dickens has also etched the incredible violence that some men turn against women. Let us recall the gruesome murder of Nancy by her "boyfriend," Bill Sikes, in *Oliver Twist*. It is this sin-ravaged caricature of man that feminists perceive, much as cynical, misanthropic men perceive the caricature of fallen Eve in women.

DISTORTION OF THE FEMALE GENIUS: THE SEDUCTRESS

As literature holds a lens to man's weaknesses, it is equally hard on woman, who has been viewed as weak, inferior, and less talented.[25] Women's defensive weapons against men have usually been depicted

---

[23] Friedrich Nietzsche, *Also sprach Zarathustra*, in Oehler, *Nietzsche-Register*, p. 71.

[24] Friedrich Nietzsche, *Jenseits von Gut und Böse*, ibid., p. 88.

[25] It is also true that the most beautiful and sublime things have been written about women from the pens of men. The most lovable characters in Shakespeare are women. Dickens etches many enchanting female characters. The same is true of the heroines of Claudel's plays. Even someone who has no great command of the literature of various countries will have no difficulty adding up hundreds of quotations that shed light on the profound understanding that some men have of the beauty and sublimity of femininity. Simone de Beauvoir, being well read, knew this, but she used *her* feminine wiles to select only quotes that buttressed her key

as wiles, duplicity, and dissimulation. She is the wily and dangerous "temptress." Her special talents and charismas, intuition, sensitivity, empathy, and tenderness have all been poisoned. Her sensitivity and tenderness degenerate into self-centeredness and sentimentality—the caricature of sensitivity, perversely enjoying one's own feelings to the total disregard of the object motivating them. Her intuition fades into wiles, and her empathy into a useful snare to catch the male sex. Telling a young girl repeatedly that she is unintelligent and untalented creates an unfavorable soil for the blossoming of her talents. Small surprise when her attention turns to a domain in which the weaker sex is definitely the stronger one—the power of attracting men for the wrong reasons.

Wiles are also tempting. Let us recall in Genesis 27 how Rebecca used deceit to guarantee that her beloved Jacob would receive Isaac's blessing. Her

---

thesis that men look down upon women or are incapable of understanding them. Referring to the fact that the most sublime characters in Paul Claudel's works are women, she claims that the saintly qualities that this great Catholic writer attributes to "the fair sex" typifies "a masculine perspective" (Simone de Beauvoir, *The Second Sex*, trans. and ed. H. M. Parshley [New York: Alfred A. Knopf, 1952; New York: Modern Library, 1968], 203). To her mind, they are left-handed compliments to make women forget that they are "forbidden" to do truly great things, the things that matter most, that is, things that put their hands at the wheel of human progress.

daughter-in-law Rachel, Jacob's beloved, stole her father's household goods without telling her husband. When Laban protested, Jacob—who did not know that Rachel had stolen them and hidden them in her camel's saddle—told him that the thief would not live. Rachel refused to be searched, alleging that "the way of women" was upon her.[26] Many of her sex have inherited this duplicity and partisanship. This is probably the most widespread censure with which men reproach women. Nietzsche claims that women have a "disgust" (*Ekel*) for truth,[27] forgetting that according to *him* there is no objective truth!

If some men can use and abuse women, then women, on the other hand, can drive men to crime. Carmen is a superb literary and musical example of a heartless woman who, using the poisonous charm of her sexual attraction, draws Jose into her nets, ruins his career, breaks the heart of his fiancée Michaela, and then, when he is totally in her power, discards him brutally. Once his passion is unleashed, the end can be foreseen. He murders her, and we cannot help but feel sorry for him.

Most exasperating of all to the misogynist, though woman is viewed as weaker than her male counterpart, she wields enormous power over him. The choice of an unworthy wife frequently leads to

---

[26] Gen 31:34–35.
[27] Nietzsche, *Menschliches*, vol. 2, in Oehler, *Nietzsche-Register*, p. 128.

dreadful consequences. Dom Prosper Guéranger writes, "When, finally, the sons of Seth took to themselves wives of the family of Cain, the human race reached the height of wickedness."[28] Later in the Bible we are told that Solomon, whose youth had been so blameless and who had been favored by God in every possible way, married foreign wives who "turned away his heart after other gods."[29] Eve brought Adam to sin. Herodias requested the beheading of Saint John the Baptist.[30] Lady Macbeth drove her husband to crime. Alas, there are and always will be Carmens in the world, as well as Pinkertons and Othellos.

A CAUTION ON GENERALIZATIONS

An important cautionary point is called for here. Generalizations are usually indicative of a mediocre mind. Sweeping statements about "all men" or "all women" are redolent of prejudice and superficiality. To call all men "predators" and all women "serpents" is as little justified as to pass negative judgment upon "all Americans," "all Jews," "all black people," or "all Hispanics." That some men are vicious and use women as plain objects of pleasure is true. That some women, conscious of their power of attracting

---

[28] Prosper Guéranger, *The Liturgical Year* (Westminster, Md.: Newman Press, 1948–1949), Monday of Septuagesima Week, 4:160.

[29] 1 Kings 11:4.

[30] Mk 6:17–29.

men, draw them into their nets while despising their prey for his weakness is also true. But it is just as true that some men are noble, chivalrous, generous, self-giving, and always ready to protect the weak. There are also women whose exquisite sensibility is put at the service of others, who joyfully forget themselves in order to cater to others' needs.

Our key thesis is that original sin has created a chasm between the two sexes and that the beautiful union intended by God to exist between them has been severely damaged. Can healing take place? Has it in fact taken place? Such questions deserve further consideration.

CHAPTER 2
The Terrible Lie of Feminism

If you want to kill a person, aim at his heart. If you want to destroy marriage, the family, the Church, and society in general, wage war on femininity. The ravages that feminism has caused can be explained only by the fact that once women are unfaithful and betray their mission, the whole of society is shaken to its very roots. If women *truly* were unimportant, insignificant, or mere "toys" for man's relaxation, the revolt triggered by the "unholy rage" of feminists could never have produced such tragic consequences.

The destruction of marriage, the family, the Church, and society is precisely the aim of contemporary feminism. The devil himself is hoisting the black flag and directing the operations. His plan of attack can be detected and counteracted only by faith, prayer, and sacrifice—in a word, only by supernatural means.

SOME CONTEMPORARY THINKERS ON FEMINISM

Before being elevated to the Chair of Saint Peter, Josef Cardinal Ratzinger—now Benedict XVI—warned the faithful of the poison contained in feminism. He names it one of the greatest dangers menacing the Church today: "I am, in fact, convinced that what feminism promotes in its radical form is no longer the Christianity that we know; it is another religion."[1] By *feminism*, as radically opposed to *femininity*, Cardinal Ratzinger is clearly referring to denigration of the great and noble role assigned to women by God. While feminism is incompatible with the Catholic view of women, the Church has always exalted womanhood in ways found only in Christian culture.

If many of us have been led to believe that the feminist movement is a legitimate response to crying injustices perpetrated against women, Donna Steichen's book *Ungodly Rage* undermines this thesis.[2] Feminism is, in fact, a radical attack on femininity. G. K. Chesterton wrote, "The Feminist . . . [is] one who dislikes the chief feminine characteristics."[3] It

---

[1] Joseph Cardinal Ratzinger with Vittorio Messori, *The Ratzinger Report: An Exclusive Interview on the State of the Church* (San Francisco: Ignatius Press, 1985), p. 97.

[2] Donna Steichen, *Ungodly Rage: The Hidden Face of Catholic Feminism* (San Francisco: Ignatius Press, 1991).

[3] G. K. Chesterton, *What's Wrong with the World* (New York: Dodd, Mead and Company, 1912), p. 223.

is because they dislike femininity that women who advocate a "unisex" mentality choose to eliminate charm, poetry, and mystery from human life. Moreover, they also wage war on the biblical teaching— "male and female he created them."[4] Feminism knowingly defies the divine plan, accusing the Creator of injustice and steering humanity in the direction of a parody of identity between male and female. How pertinent in response is Chesterton's remark that there is nothing more opposed to equality than identity. Let us suppose that boxing matches were introduced between men and women. Feminists would take to the streets to protest male brutality. Yet, according to their views, it would be promoting equality.

Today, women ape male attire. Women copy male behavior—many have taught themselves to drink like men, to curse like men, to smoke cigars like men, and to imitate slavishly all the least attractive characteristics of the stronger sex. This in turn encourages men to abandon the chivalrous traditions prevalent in the past, to replace them with a chumminess that opens the door to vulgarity. Chesterton expressed this truth in his own inimitable fashion: "I remember an artistic and eager lady asking me . . . whether I believed in comradeship between the sexes and why not." Chesterton responded, "Because if I were to treat you for two

---

[4] Gen 1:27.

minutes like a comrade you would turn me out of the house."[5]

A man responds to a woman either with respect or with contempt, either with reverence or with lust, not with a sense of identity. Women have the power to draw out of men what is best in them and kindle purity in their souls or to awaken what is worst in them and fuel in them the ever-present furnace of lust.[6] A man who sees a woman whose body language expresses holy modesty, which is not to be confused with prudishness, will inevitably feel awe in front of her and will understand that her very presence calls him to adopt a reverent attitude. A woman whose body language expresses shamelessness and vulgarity, on the other hand, actually invites the men who approach her to have unchaste thoughts and to exhibit coarse behavior.

In Raïssa Maritain's diary, we find the following words: "All women should meditate on Saint Paul's Epistle to Timothy, in which he admonishes women to 'adorn themselves modestly.'"[7] He is referring to a secret confided to women, and this secret calls for holy *pudeur*.[8] Alas, this sensibility for the mystery of femi-

---

[5] Chesterton, *What's Wrong with the World*, p. 176.

[6] Raïssa Maritain, *Raïssa's Journal*, presented by Jacques Maritain (Albany, N.Y.: Magi Books, 1974).

[7] 1 Tim 2:9; Maritain, *Raïssa's Journal*.

[8] A French word that means reverence for something that is mysterious and sacred that, because of its personal and intimate character, calls for veiling.

ninity is so lost today that even many pious and good young girls seem totally unaware that their way of dressing, their way of sitting, their posture, their body language, are often incompatible with their calling.

That feminism had already spread its tentacles in Denmark, a Protestant country, is proven by what Kierkegaard wrote:

> I hate all talk about the emancipation of woman. God forbid that ever it may come to pass. I cannot tell you with what pain this thought is able to pierce my heart, nor what passionate exasperation, what hate I feel toward every one who gives vent to such talk.... No base seducer could think out a more dangerous doctrine for woman, for once he has made her believe this, she is entirely in his power, at the mercy of his will, she can be nothing for man, except a prey to his whims, whereas as woman she can be everything for him.[9]

Dostoyevsky defends a similar thesis: "I assure you all this women question has been invented for them by men in foolishness and to their own hurt."[10] In other words, if the admirable complementarity of men and women is abolished, disastrous consequences will follow not only for the "fair sex" but for men as well.

---

[9] Søren Kierkegaard, *Either/Or: A Fragment of Life*, trans. Walter Lowrie (Princeton, N.J.: Princeton University Press, 1944), pp. 260, 261.

[10] Fyodor Dostoyevsky, *The Possessed* (New York: Dell Publishing, 1961), p. 414.

Chesterton formulates a similar thought when he writes, "I would give woman, not more rights, but more privileges."[11] He also writes that "I am not satisfied with the statement that my daughter must have unwomanly powers because she has unwomanly wrongs."[12] Joseph Pearce writes that one of Solzhenitsyn's key ideas is that "love without the spiritual side is not love." Pearce writes further, "Linked with this spiritual dimension was the characterization of the female characters in the book [*The Cancer Ward*] who are developed with strength and sympathy but in an implicitly anti-feminist, although not anti-feminine, direction."[13] "I do feel that feminism is anti-natural," Solzhenitsyn asserted. "It does destroy the feminine and in so doing it also destroys humankind. It disassembles the female side of humankind and the male side also suffers. This is one of the manifestations of the fact that people have lost the high image of man as a creation of God. Instead we have this unbridled, almost frenzied, moving about of liberalism which fails to understand human nature itself, not just the feminine, but human existence, being blinded by this wild, liberal dancing."[14]

---

[11] Chesterton, *What's Wrong with the World*, p. 222.

[12] Ibid., p. 224.

[13] Joseph Pearce, *Solzhenitsyn: A Soul in Exile* (Grand Rapids, Mich.: Baker Books, 2001), p. 306.

[14] Ibid.

Nietzsche argues that "an instinctive hatred of the woman who is a failure" originates the fraudulent call for "liberation" of women.[15] He perceives clearly that feminism is nothing else than the masculinization of women.[16] The very same thinker has also diagnosed that feminism is the enemy of femininity. He writes, "Since the French Revolution, woman's influence has decreased in the very proportion that her rights and her pretensions have increased."[17] Much as one is right to reject Nietzsche's philosophy, it cannot be denied that he can be remarkably perceptive. A woman's power lies not so much in asserting herself as in being what she is called upon to be.

This importance to humanity of simple feminine being is the very clear message that Solzhenitsyn transmitted in writing *Matryona's House*, which was, of course, refused publication in Soviet Russia, as clearly a threat to the atheistic state. This admirable short story depicts the life of a "nobody," a poor old woman who is looked down upon by everyone but who turns out to be a heroine who sheds light that blinds those unworthy to tie her shoelaces. Her Christian heart illuminates the squalor in which she lives. Yet, Solzhenitsyn writes, "none of us who

---

[15] Friedrich Nietzsche, *Ecce Homo*, "Warum ich so gute Bücher schreibe" [Why I write such good books], no. 5.

[16] Friedrich Nietzsche, *Die Unschuld des Werdens*, p. 311.

[17] Friedrich Nietzsche, *Aphorismes*, no. 6071.

lived close to her perceived that she was the one righteous person without whom, as the saying goes, no city can stand. Neither can the whole world."[18]

From another angle, the sculptor Adolf von Hildebrand hints at the crucial complementarity of men and women. Without feminine contact, men will never develop their "human side." They become inventors, creators, and producers, but their own being remains an uncultivated field. Von Hildebrand tacitly agrees with Chesterton's remark that men under such conditions are tempted to fly into abstractions. A liberal Protestant, in fact a noble pagan and a reverent pantheist, he writes the following lines: "So it is that we love a woman as our holy ghost; through womanhood we develop our most human element into full sensibility; the rest of our being belongs therefore to the outer world."[19] In other words, when complementarity of men and women is denied, humanity enters a lopsided relation with the material world.

THE WAR ON FEMININITY

Our society is waging war on femininity. Let me state emphatically that the modern world of machines and techniques is a world in which, by its very being, the

---

[18] Aleksandr Isaevich Solzhenitsyn, *Matryona's House, and Other Stories*, trans. Michael Glenny (Harmondsworth, U.K.: Penguin Books, 1975).

[19] Harry Brewster, *The Cosmopolites* (Norwich, U.K.: Michael Russell, 1994), p. 139.

feminine element is systematically eliminated. The remarkable book by Karl Stern *The Flight from Woman* is a perfect diagnosis of this dangerous situation.[20] Even the manner in which contemporary man expresses himself betrays this hostility. Acronyms replace words. For the uninitiated, it is often difficult to understand the jargon of journalists and news anchors. The acronyms FBI, CIA, and IRS are familiar enough, but innumerable other examples are as foreign to us as Chinese. One writer so desperately wanted to prove his originality and "creativity" that he wrote a novel in which most objects were identified by chemical formulas. Water, for example, was H_2O. He certainly succeeded in being "original," but how many people read his book, despite its being recommended as an aid for insomnia?

How right Gertrud von le Fort was when she wrote, "Materialism, socialism, futurism have a masculine connotation. They are no longer in the fullest sense organic creations from a totality of polaric powers. . . . Mysteries are no longer needed."[21] Feminism has ironically succeeded in securing a great masculine victory. Our world has become dominated by machines, technology, and mind-boggling scientific discoveries, where telephone, radio, television,

---

[20] Karl Stern, *The Flight from Woman* (New York: Paragon House, 1986).

[21] Gertrud von le Fort, *The Eternal Woman* (Milwaukee: Bruce Publishing Co., 1954), p. 46. Karl Stern's book *Flight from Woman* is devoted to this theme.

fax machines, and e-mail more and more replace personal contacts—which are the feminine forte. One would expect intelligent women to understand that the call of the hour is to counteract this soulless technology by emphasizing the female element: the personal, the living, the concrete, the heart. Here the foolishness of feminists becomes apparent—they do the very opposite.

While this masculinized modern technology has brought great material wealth, it has also created new and terrible human deprivations. There is first the deprivation of deep thought. Why did linguistic philosophy, a philosophical approach that eliminates the crucial concerns of the human mind and the human heart, make headlines early in the twentieth century? This fashionable philosophy has no concern for the basic questions to which the French philosopher Jacques Chevalier refers, the set of questions every man raises when he faces death. Once again, Platonic wisdom is a source of awe. Plato tells us that ignorance of the highest things was the cause of the ruin of the Dorian power: "That was then, and is still, and always will be the case."[22] What matters most, he writes, "is the knowledge of the gods . . . one of the noblest sources of knowledge."[23]

---

[22] Plato, *The Laws*, trans. Benjamin Jowett (New York: Cosimo, 2008), no. 688, p. 65.
[23] Ibid., no. 966, p. 302.

Then there is the deprivation of symbolism. Von le Fort has understood how impoverishing it is when abstract thinking eliminates the language of physical symbols.[24] In the traditional Mass, for example, the priest was facing east. East is symbolic of the rising sun; it is appropriate because Christ is the sun of creation. The faithful received Holy Communion kneeling, for this is a posture symbolic of adoration. The results of abolishing these rich symbols have been disastrous and have led many to lose their understanding of transcendent realities.

There is the deprivation of nurturing love. C. S. Lewis was keenly aware of this deprivation of affectivity when he wrote, "The task of the modern educator is not to cut down jungles but to irrigate deserts."[25] It should surprise no one that the great sickness of our rich society is despair, though our despair is covered by the deafening noise of our machinery. Is it surprising that one of the most popular discoveries of modern psychology is the "deprivation syndrome," the sad acknowledgment that people are starving because they have been deprived of love? Love that is the right of every child. Once marriages break down, families become cancerous. When most small children have a television, a baby computer, and a telephone, how many

---

[24] Von le Fort, *Eternal Woman*, XIII.
[25] C. S. Lewis, *The Abolition of Man* (New York: Collier Books, 1962), p. 24.

of them are hugged, told that they are loved? Why is it that so many men in our society have a deadly fear of any affectivity and commitment? The best among them may date a girl for years and enjoy being with her . . . but never ask her to marry him. Commitment is in mourning.

There is the deprivation of silence. Silence, that balm of the soul, has been scientifically ostracized, and for good reason—to prevent us from thinking. In relating the miraculous story of his conversion, Father Douglas Calloway relates that the first time he experienced "silence," he was *terrified*. In that moment, he was forced to face himself in all his filth.

There is the deprivation of personal contact. A sojourn in contemporary hospitals makes one experience that the personal contact between the physician and the patient is rationed to a minimum. Most of the "work" is done by machines. When I was a child in Belgium, it was done through the tender care of nursing sisters. We live in a world that has become more and more dehumanized, more and more heartless, a world dominated by technology, by machines. Their dehumanized designs embody the worst stereotypes of a godless masculinity. The machines cannot smile or utter a word of comfort to the sick, who are desperately in need of understanding, patience, and compassion in order to carry well the cross of physical and psychological suffering. Human persons are made of body and soul, and the body cannot recover when the soul is neglected. Blessed Teresa of Calcutta said that spiritual destitution is more detrimental to man than acute physical misery. Clearly, technology has its merits and is not to be abandoned; but unless it is complemented by the female element of empathy, it will have disastrous effects.

Empathy is the special charisma of women and particularly of women religious, who, in the past when their role was predominant in hospitals, gave joy and comfort to those afflicted. As a side note, today men have entered into this field that was the privilege of women. Recently I had the experience of having male nurses. Frankly, being men, many lack the personal touch that is the secret of true women. Moreover, in a field such as nursing, they can make inappropriate remarks that betray a total lack of reverence toward women patients. A helpless female patient calls for special respect.

Today's climate not only discourages religious vocations but actually offers a strong incentive to encourage nuns to quit their habit and to turn to occupations that are "more productive." Feminists proclaim that only masculine occupations are fulfilling. Unless we abandon what Karl Stern calls "the flight from woman," our amazing technological advances will be our spiritual downfall. We desperately need both the masculine and the feminine element. They complement each other. They belong together.

How right Chesterton was when he wrote, "I want to destroy the tyranny. They [the feminists] want to destroy the womanhood."[26] This assertion buttresses the thesis we shall defend, namely, that a man worthy of this name understands women much better than they can be understood by other women, even though they are "on the same side of the fence" and therefore share experiences totally foreign to the other sex. Dietrich von Hildebrand writes, "The fact that the two natures are ordered towards each other enables an understanding of each other of the deepest kind."[27] It is my claim that in order for a woman truly to understand the beauty of masculinity, she must first completely understand and gratefully accept her femininity. This is why the sweet Theotokos[28] understood and loved Christ most.

More and more women are now entering fields that once were the domain of men, just as men are now entering fields traditionally reserved to women. This is justifiable in some cases. There are women who are competent in "male" fields and men who discharge what were once viewed as "female" activities extremely well. However, many women in our society have become disciples of Esau, who gave up his birthright for a mess of pottage.

---

[26] Chesterton, *What's Wrong with the World*, p. 225.

[27] Dietrich von Hildebrand, *Man and Woman: Love and the Meaning of Intimacy* (Chicago: Franciscan Herald Press, 1966), p. 65.

[28] *Theotokos* means "Mother of God" (literally, "God-bearer").

Chesterton perceived the danger of devaluing a woman's specifically feminine contributions: "How can it be broad to be the same thing to everyone, and narrow to be everything to someone?"[29] What does a woman sacrifice in order to be a transitory minister of state? Statistics tell us that career women—if they decide to get married—get married late and then either do not become mothers or have children at an age when their physical resiliency is on the decline. The West is dying out for want of babies; elderly people live longer and longer, creating a serious imbalance between youth and old age that rightly worries the economists. This is only a social and economic problem, but it shows that the feminist abandonment of the home has consequences that might be viewed as immanent punishments.

Feminists forget that *sub specie aeternitatis* (under the aspect of eternity) to be wife and mother, to create a "home," to "be there," to give love, and to listen to the woes of little ones (and not-so-little ones) who crave for tenderness and affection is like being the sun illuminating a dark world. There are millions of children in our society who are disturbed because they are the victims of a motherless (and fatherless) youth. A mother can shed more light and warmth in our sad world when she nurses a baby than when she is engaged in gigantic political

---

[29] Chesterton, *What's Wrong with the World*, p. 165.

ventures—most of which center around the art of doubtful compromises.

There are always, of course, extraordinary callings, but we should not forget that they are exceptions. Joan of Arc, one of the greatest generals that ever lived, did not choose to command an army. Furthermore, she paid a heavy price for her obedience to her extraordinary calling. Quite a few women might think that they are potential Joans, but most are victims of self-aggrandizement and wishful thinking. How wise Plato was when he wrote that those truly worthy to be leaders will not be anxious to head the state. "[They] will take office as a stern necessity."[30] They should not covet the task.

THE WAR ON POETRY AND BEAUTY

In waging war on femininity, the modern world has also chosen to wage war on poetry. Men have been the great poets, but much of their work has been inspired by women. Dante's Beatrice is their queen, but there are quite a few princesses, duchesses, and countesses who, on a more modest plane, have inspired the genius of a receptive, poetic man. Such women have the talent to spread the perfume of poetry in their home. A woman's sensitivity is both

---

[30] Plato, *The Republic*, in *The Dialogues of Plato*, trans. B. Jowett, 3rd ed., vol. 3 (Oxford: Clarendon Press, 1892), no. 520, p. 221.

her strength and her weakness, depending upon whether her heart is purified or has fallen into the nets of sentimentality and partisanship. Dante and not Beatrice wrote the *Divine Comedy*, but she inspired the greatest work of Catholic poetry. His love for her made him promise to write a work dedicated to her praise, a work that would surpass whatever had been written before. He kept his word. Had Beatrice been a feminist, I have my doubts that she could have kindled Dante's genius.

Few women write poems; many "live" poetry. That women can inspire their husbands while remaining in the background is proven by reading the eulogy given them in hundreds of prefaces. The South African poet Roy Campbell writes that his wife Mary's help was "invaluable" to his work. "She is the perfect model of what an artist's wife should be. But I get all the damned credit for it."[31] This encomium is not a rare phenomenon; but a loving wife, far from claiming any credit, chooses to avoid the limelight. Nietzsche refers to this phenomenon but, as expected, adds a drop of poison when he writes that women are willing *Opfertiere* (sacrificial

---

[31] Roy Campbell, unpublished letter to C. J. Sibbett, late November or early December 1926, quoted in Joseph Pearce, *Unafraid of Virginia Woolf: The Friends and Enemies of Roy Campbell* (Wilmington, Del.: ISI Books, 2004), p. 100. (Originally published as *Bloomsbury and Beyond: The Friends and Enemies of Roy Campbell* [London: HarperCollins Publishers, 2001].)

animals) of famous men.[32] Simone de Beauvoir—and this is the peak of irony for this doctrinaire feminist—sacrificed her passionate love affair with the American writer Nelson Algren, leaving Chicago against his will, upon receiving a message that the writer Jean-Paul Sartre needed her help.

Physical perceptions of beauty are crucial for our spiritual life, as Plato saw centuries ago, because we are made of body and soul. How right he was when he stressed the importance of exposing children to true beauty, writing, "Then will our youth dwell in a land of health, amid fair sights and sounds, and receive the good in everything; and beauty, the effluence of fair works, shall flow into the eye and ear, like a health-giving breeze from a purer region, and insensibly draw the soul from earliest years into likeness and sympathy with the beauty of reason."[33]

Modern architecture and modern churches have no soul. In some way, one could say that we are practicing the cult of ugliness. The danger of getting used to ugliness is great, and it is saddening that the danger either is not recognized, not properly diagnosed, or underestimated. Since Vatican II, many of our magnificent churches, which were a rich dowry left to us by the faith of our ancestors, have been stripped of their beauty. Altar rails of great artistry

---

[32] Friedrich Nietzsche, *Menschliches, Allzumenschliches*, vol. 1, no. 430.

[33] Plato, *The Republic*, no. 401d.

have been destroyed with iconoclastic rage, even though there is not a single word in the documents of Vatican II commanding these barbaric "sins." Priests in some countries threw precious religious objects from their churches into the streets, sniffing that they no longer "reflected the spirit of the time."

THE WAR ON SPIRITUAL ECOLOGY

Today, we are so bewitched by our mind-boggling technical accomplishments that we forget what matters most is warmth of heart. The danger is great. The balance between masculinity and femininity is, from the point of view of "spiritual ecology," of capital importance. This was admirably perceived by Pope Benedict XVI when he was Cardinal Ratzinger. During an interview with Vittorio Messori, he deplored the prevalent masculine trend in our society to embrace the "cult" of efficiency.[34] Needless to say, it is efficiency stripped of holiness.[35]

One speaks so much about ecological sins. Nature is being brutally and meaninglessly destroyed, and, without being "green," one must admit that respect for the beauty of nature and its message is often disregarded for the sake of financial profits. More importantly, though, how can one close one's eyes to

---

[34] Ratzinger, *Ratzinger Report*, p. 99.
[35] See Dietrich von Hildebrand, "Efficiency and Holiness," in *The New Tower of Babel* (New York: P. J. Kenedy and Sons, 1953), pp. 205–43.

a danger that is much more serious: the war waged on femininity? Each sex has its role; each has its talents; each has its mission. To create a "sexless" society is to destroy the ecological design of the human being and will inevitably lead to religious, moral, psychological, and physical disasters.

To advocate new families made up of two fathers or two mothers must, to use the strong language of Léon Bloy, make the stars bellow. It is metaphysically impossible for two men or two women to complete each other, for the very plain reason that they have the same sex. A denial of the basic metaphysical truth found in Genesis is an act of rebellion that is bound to have tragic consequences. Great and admirable as true friendship between women or between men can be, it can never be a substitute for the admirable complementarity that God established between Adam and Eve. To deny this obvious truth is an abomination. We shall pay the price by creating a society in which madness is praised as a sign of "progress," the fruit of "scientific" discoveries—a society in which madness is politically correct.

To advocate new families made up of two fathers or two mothers will, one day, lead to the claim that the U.S. Constitution sees no difference between male and female. There is no logical termination to the elimination of old—and valuable—taboos. *Progress* is an equivocal word, naïvely identified with improvement. It means only "to go forward," though; and to go forward toward an abyss is certainly not desirable. Scientific discoveries, however impressive, can never decide what is morally right or wrong. Science's horizon is always limited to the physical universe and cannot pontificate in the moral or spiritual domains, in which it is totally incompetent. An anthropologist is not equipped to write on ethics. He can give us facts about the material universe, but he cannot tell us how men should behave. When we become confused about these truths, we sow seeds of death.

SUPERNATURAL BLINDNESS: TRIUMPHANT SECULARISM

Original sin has blinded men to the beauty of the supernatural. Secular "values" can, therefore, mistakenly gain pride of place. Strength, physical beauty, success, power—all of which Plato calls "human goods," as opposed to "divine goods," such as goodness per se[36]—are what most people crave. "Self-fulfillment" is the slogan of the new aristocracy, and our secularized society teaches us to strive for it.

One of the key marks of secularism is its denial of any transcendence. It understands the world in which we live as the only valid reality. Consequently, producing, inventing, accomplishing, improving, and changing seem more important than "being." This is

---

[36] Plato, *The Laws*, no. 631.

at loggerheads with the fundamental Christian principle that what matters most is not what one produces, but what one is as a person. Love, generosity, purity, moral courage, humility, and similar virtues are precious in God's sight and have, to borrow words from Kierkegaard, an "eternal resonance."

In his great book *The Lord*, Romano Guardini writes, "Christianity has always placed the life struggling for inner truth and ultimate love above that intent on exterior action, even the most courageous and excellent. It has always valued silence more highly than words, purity of intent more than success, the magnanimity of love more than the effect of labor."[37]

CONCLUSION

This leads us back to our key thesis. Original sin has created a chasm between the two sexes. The beautiful union meant by God to exist between man and woman has been severely shattered and definitely calls for healing. Can this healing take place? Has it in fact taken place? This is the question we will address in the next chapter.

---

[37] Romano Guardini, *The Lord* (Washington, D.C.: Gateway Editions, 1996), p. 227.

CHAPTER 3
The Feminine Genius: Mystery, Veiling, Piety, and Modesty

Women are definitely more mysterious than men, not primarily because their affective life is more complex and subtle, but especially because there is *something in woman that calls for veiling*. It is not by accident that women traditionally wore a veil in Catholic churches. This custom was deeply symbolic, but alas, this symbolism has now been lost. Under the influence of feminism, many Catholics were led to believe that veiling indicated some sort of inferiority and therefore abandoned the practice.

This last interpretation rests on a misunderstanding. Far from indicating inferiority, the veil points to sacredness. While we cover what is ugly, unattractive, or repulsive, we veil what is sacred, mysterious, and sublime. When Moses came down from Mount Sinai, he veiled his face to hide the glow that shone from him after God had deigned to speak with him. Moses' veiling reflected the mystery and depth of his experience in talking with God.

Every woman carries within herself a secret, something mysterious and sacred. This secret is, on the natural level, the potential of new life. Adam called Eve "the mother of the living" because life begins in the mystery of the female body, not in the male semen. It begins in the fecundated egg, hidden in the temple of her body. When the female egg has been fertilized, God "touches" the female body to create a child's soul. In this creation, neither father nor mother have any part, but because the baby's soul is infused within the woman's body, there is a closeness between the mother and her Creator that has no duplicate in fatherhood. Her body, touched by God Himself, becomes a sacred ground.

That is why the way that a woman dresses, the way she sits, walks, or laughs should always be stamped by a note of holy reserve. A woman, conscious of her unmerited privilege, will necessarily adopt a bodily posture—a "body language"—that adequately reflects this calling.

Woman and mystery are so closely linked that only those who have opted for willful blindness cannot perceive that veiling and femininity essentially belong together. Von le Fort writes, "[C]ertain fashions become monstrous traitors. . . . To unveil her [the woman] means to destroy her mystery."¹ Saint Paul urges women to dress with modesty.² How one wishes that young girls today would be reminded of this noble teaching that would shelter them from tragic experiences that often ruin their lives!

A woman fulfills her awesome mission not through exterior accomplishments but through prayer, sacrifice, and love. Women are notoriously more pious than men. One needs only to visit churches, particularly in Latin countries, to see that women outnumber men. It is a well-known fact that whatever faith was kept in Soviet Russia was safeguarded by women.³ Around 1900, the French Academy offered an award to the person who best answered the following question: "Why are there more men than women in jail?" The award was given to the person who wrote, "Because there are more women than men in churches."

Women are more pious than men because they are more receptive, and receptivity is the road to holiness. One reaches holiness not by efficiency (an American ideal) but by total acceptance of God's will, by giving a total Yes to His plans for us. All the

---

[1] Gertrud von le Fort, *The Eternal Woman* (Milwaukee: Bruce Publishing Co., 1954), p. 11.

[2] 1 Tim 2:9.

[3] Paul Evdokimov, *Woman and the Salvation of the World: A Christian Anthropology on the Charisms of Women*, trans. Anthony P. Gythiel (Crestwood, N.Y.: St. Vladimir's Seminary Press, 1994), p. 267.

Holy Virgin did was to say, "I am the handmaid of the Lord; let it be done to me according to your word."[4] Saint Augustine expresses a similar thought when he writes, "Da quod jubes et jube quod vis" (Give what you command, and then command what you will).[5] He is asking the Lord first to make him *receptive* to His gift; that will, in turn, enable him to fulfill all His holy commands. All a creature aiming at holiness needs to do is to say yes. Both the Old and the New Testament highlight this truth. The little Samuel, when hearing God's voice in the temple, answered only, "Speak, for thy servant hears."[6]

The male temptation to value activism and uncontemplative creativity—while denigrating receptivity—was a temptation unfelt by most women until feminism convinced some of them that productivity, activity, and so-called creativity is what matters most in life. This belief goes so far that in our society it now matters little what one creates (whether beautiful or ugly, intelligent or stupid) as long as one can claim creativity. This is a heresy that has been condemned under the name of Americanism.

When piety dies out in women, society is threatened in its very fabric, for woman's relationship to the sacred keeps the Church and society on an even keel. When this link is severed, both are threatened

---

[4] Lk 1:38.

[5] Augustine, *Confessions*, bk. 10, no. 40.

[6] 1 Sam 3:10.

by moral chaos. Atheism is particularly discordant in a woman as, analogously, it is particularly out of tune in the Chosen People. Raïssa Maritain writes in her diary: "*Pudeur* is commonly more accentuated in woman because woman is to some extent above and below animal nature: above, by the greater purity of her life—I am speaking in general;—below, because her maternal functions are vegetative rather than animal.[7] For these two reasons it is more repugnant for her to be recalled to her carnal functions."[8]

The ravages that feminism is creating in our society can hardly be gauged. Poisoned by a wrong philosophy, millions of women now trample upon the mystery of their femininity and willingly collaborate with men in committing one of the most horrendous of all crimes, the murder of the defenseless unborn child. Terrible as the crime of the abortionist is, the crime of the one aborting is truly unfathomable; the woman not only assists in a murder but

---

[7] Here Maritain means that the manner and timing of the growth of the baby in a woman's womb is beyond her interior control once fecundation has occurred. It is something that happens to her rather than something she enacts.

[8] Raïssa Maritain, *Raïssa's Journal*, presented by Jacques Maritain (Albany, N.Y.: Magi Books, 1974), pp. 94–95. Jacques Maritain adds in a footnote: "Raïssa wrote these lines in 1919. After the second world war she might have added (it is something she often said to me) that when woman thinks she has emancipated herself by rejecting what is characteristic of her nature 'in general', her immodesty becomes worse than that of man."

betrays her very vocation to give life, becoming instead the apostle of death. Even though all of us are aware of the tragic situations in which young, immature girls find themselves, psychologists and priests know that when they have aborted, it will be very difficult for them to recover.

In *The Scarlet Letter* by Nathaniel Hawthorne, the heroine Hester Prynne, mother of an illegitimate child, is condemned to carry the letter A (for *adulteress*) on her bosom to make everyone aware of her shame and invite them to show contempt for her degradation. The history of mankind testifies to the fact that women were usually much more severely censured than men for a sin that, by its very nature, calls for two partners. Men are often excused for their unchaste behavior because it is seen as "in their nature," and "they must sow their wild oats." Women, on the other hand, are just as often treated with inhuman severity for the same failing. Obviously, fornication and adultery are of equal moral gravity, whether committed by a man or by a woman. The social censures to which we have alluded, however, indicate that deep down, societies acknowledge the fact that women—having received a sacred calling—are particularly accountable for any deviation from this noble vocation. Unchaste behavior on the part of a woman amounts to a betrayal of a trust given to her by God. For this reason, impure women were, and are, looked down upon as contemptible, despicable, and shameful, and often in the most ruthless and uncharitable ways. (Today the tendency is to show indifference or compassion toward such women, but unfortunately this often reflects the view that sins of the flesh are not grave offenses against God.)

No doubt, a woman is more deeply affected by unchaste behavior than is a man. The enamel of her soul is more severely scratched by this type of sin than is his, for a man can better separate his mind from his heart and usually does not surrender himself in the same fashion. This capacity to divorce mind and emotions is both an advantage and a disadvantage. It is expedient when there is need for an objective judgment. It also points, however, to a dichotomy in a man's soul that can be healed only by a deep religious life, especially by a deep devotion to Mary.

FECUNDITY

It cannot be emphasized enough that the admirable complementarity existing between men and women is not only biological but also psychological, intellectual, affective, spiritual, and religious. Dietrich von Hildebrand writes:

> The spiritual contact of man and woman also has a positive mission, namely the unique stimulation and spiritual fecundation. Particular virtues in both are awakened which otherwise remain undeveloped.

> The chivalrous attitude awakens in the man a stronger self-control, a more humble attitude, a greater delicacy and purity, a certain melting and enlivening of his nature. With the woman, on the other hand, a widening of her intellect takes place, a broader and more principle-tied foundation for her sense of values, a noble reserve on one hand, and a special warmth and devotion on the other, appears.[9]

Adolf von Hildebrand, whom we have quoted before, makes a similar point: "So it is that we love a woman as our holy ghost; through womanhood we develop our most human element into full sensibility; the rest of our being belongs therefore to the outer world."[10] His reference to the Holy Ghost clearly indicates his ignorance of the supernatural; nonetheless, he timidly hints at the spiritual role women should play in a man's life.

Man fecundates woman biologically. Woman can fecundate man intellectually and spiritually. When a woman's heart is purified by true love, she possesses "holy tools" that will enable her, by her very being, to have a redeeming influence on men. This is a theme that the young Kierkegaard, in love with Regina Olsen, has admirably sketched in volume 2 of *Either/Or*. He writes, "[O]ut of a hundred

---

[9] Dietrich von Hildebrand, *Man and Woman: Love and the Meaning of Intimacy* (Chicago: Franciscan Herald Press, 1966), pp. 64–65.

[10] Harry Brewster, *The Cosmopolites* (Norwich, U.K.: Michael Russell, 1994), p. 139.

men who go astray in the world ninety and nine are saved by women and one by immediate divine grace."[11] He clearly means to say that grace often works *through women*. Divine grace brought Augustine into the Holy Catholic Church, but his mother Monica played a crucial role as instrument of this grace. The point that Kierkegaard wishes to make is that the role of women is essentially ethical and religious. In the words of Chesterton, "Cleverness shall be left for men and wisdom for women."[12] This is what Dietrich von Hildebrand calls "the apostolate of being."[13]

Just as a man's mind can fecundate a woman's mind, female intuition can benefit man's creativity. Rightly, Chesterton remarks that "men are all theoretical,"[14] but theories should be checked against concrete reality. Abstractions can cut one off from the facts of everyday life. Once again, it is worth quoting him: "The mind that finds its way to wild places is the poet's; but the mind that never finds its way back is the lunatic's."[15] This is when a man

---

[11] Søren Kierkegaard, *Either/Or: A Fragment of Life*, trans. Walter Lowrie (Princeton, N.J.: Princeton University Press, 1944), 2:174.

[12] G. K. Chesterton, *What's Wrong with the World* (New York: Dodd, Mead and Company, 1912), p. 156. As Chesterton remarks, when men want to be impressive, they wear skirts (p. 185).

[13] Unpublished remark often mentioned in his talks.

[14] Chesterton, *What's Wrong with the World*, p. 117.

[15] Ibid., p. 161.

desperately needs a wise woman to "bring him back." Some men are such passionate chess players that they totally lose contact with concrete reality. It is hard to imagine that a woman could fall into this tempting but inhuman trap.

Too often, men identify reason with a cold, rationalistic interpretation of life. This caricature of reason is ossified and flounders into abstractions that inevitably will leave him starving. The great Cardinal Newman was aware of this danger when he wrote, "I was beginning to prefer intellectual excellence to moral; I was drifting in the direction of liberalism."[16] One of the greatest masters of the spiritual life, Dom Lorenzo Scupoli, writes, "It is much more difficult to remedy pride of the understanding than that of the heart."[17] Like Cardinal Newman before him, Chesterton is keenly aware of the grave dangers confronting "intellectuals," that is, those who suffer from a hypertrophy of the mind and an atrophy of the heart. This is why he laments the fact that "a large section of the Intelligentsia seemed wholly devoid of Intelligence."[18] All the "big" errors, all the most deplorable heresies, have

---

[16] John Henry Cardinal Newman, *Apologia pro Vita Sua* (London: George Routledge and Sons), pp. 15–16.

[17] Dom Lorenzo Scupoli, *The Spiritual Combat and a Treatise on Peace of Soul* (Rockford, Ill.: TAN Books and Publishers, 1945), p. 24.

[18] G. K. Chesterton, *The Autobiography of G. K. Chesterton* (San Francisco: Ignatius Press, 2006), p. 156.

been produced by "intellectuals." He also writes: "True as it is that a woman's mind needs to be guided by a man's intellect—for if carried by her unsanctioned emotions, she can easily stray in her reasoning—it is just as true that a woman's intuition can enrich a man's mind. Even Nietzsche [in "The Innocence of Becoming"] has words of praise for a woman's remarkable subtlety of her instinct."[19]

The woman is characterized by a close meld of mind and heart.[20] It is both her strength and her weakness, depending, as always, upon whether her heart is purified or has been poisoned by sentimentality and partisanship. Love teaches a woman worthy of the name to be "flexible." Once again, Chesterton has formulated this with his usual wit: "Much of what is called her subservience and even her pliability is merely the subservience and pliability of a universal remedy; she varies as medicines vary, with the disease. She has to be an optimist to the morbid husband, a salutary pessimist to the happy-go-lucky husband. She has to prevent the Quixote from being put upon, and the bully from putting upon others."[21]

In his beautiful biography of Saint Francis, Johannes Jörgensen writes the following words:

---

[19] This is a good example of what I dub "the privilege of geniuses" to contradict themselves. Nietzsche is known to write horrible things about women and later praise them highly.

[20] Von Hildebrand, *Man and Woman*, p. 63.

[21] Chesterton, *What's Wrong with the World*, pp. 161–62.

"While men sometimes must be satisfied to represent theory, practice, often outside of all theory, is the vocation of woman. No one ever realizes more fully a man's ideal than a woman, once she is possessed by it."[22] In these words, the Danish convert hints at the beautiful complementarity of men and women. Men create and invent; women live. Women want theories to be "incarnated" and concretely realized, provided they are worth realizing. Saint Edith Stein said something similar in a talk she delivered at Salzburg in 1930. She rightly insists that women are more concerned about persons than about impersonal things, more interested in the concrete than in the abstract, and more centered on the living than on the nonliving.[23]

In the wake of Vatican II, quite a few "intellectuals" lost their footing, carried away by the modernist tsunami that took place. Several of them found their way back, thanks to their wives, as they like to acknowledge publicly: William Coulson and William May, who both signed the document in the *New York Times* rejecting *Humanae Vitae* in 1968, come to mind.[24]

---

[22] Johannes Jörgensen, *Saint Francis of Assisi: A Biography*, trans. T. O'Conor Sloane (New York: Longmans, Green, and Co., 1912), p. 122.

[23] J. Oesterreicher, *Walls Are Crumbling: Seven Jewish Philosophers Discover Christ* (London: Devin-Adair, 1952), p. 326.

[24] Soon after the publication of *Humanae Vitae* in July 1968, very many Catholics (both theologians and philosophers)

A woman's mission is not primarily intellectual or creative. *It is essentially spiritual and religious.* Both Gertrud von le Fort and Paul Evdokimov defend this thesis. A woman is meant to be a religious magnet, and when she betrays her mission, the sun sets. Evdokimov writes, *"In the spiritual domain, it is the woman who is the stronger sex."*[25] He writes further that it is spiritual maternity that gives birth to Christ in human beings, through the power of the Holy Spirit.[26] Pascal is clearly referring to this spiritual power when he wrote the profound words, "The heart has its reasons, which reason does not know."[27] Roy Campbell expresses a similar thought in a letter written to his wife, Mary. He writes: "I am sick of hanging about without you and Tessy. All the lovely things I see are only half as lovely as they would be if you were here to share them. You have taught me to look at things in the same way as you do and I do miss half their beauty when you're not there. D'you remember when I used to laugh at you

---

protested the encyclical. They chose to do this publicly with an ad in the *New York Times*. The ad covered an entire page in order to include all of the names. William May, and many others, later regretted their action.

[25] Evdokimov, *Woman and the Salvation of the World*, p. 157. Emphasis in original.

[26] Ibid., p. 222.

[27] Blaise Pascal, *Pensées*, trans. W. F. Trotter (New York: E. P. Dutton, 1958; Mineola, N.Y.: Dover Publications, 2003), no. 277, p. 78.

for raving about sunsets etc. I always had the logic on my side but you had something stronger."[28]

That women have a mission to awaken a "human side" in men—who are always tempted to lose touch with the concrete—is acknowledged by *truly* great men. The weaker sex has the mission to "humanize" men. Chesterton speaks of "the savage common sense" of the weaker sex and adds wisely that "if men were to live without women, they must not live without rules."[29] This is a piece of wisdom that explains why the Rule of Saint Benedict was made strict. Father Bouyer chimes in and writes, "There is, therefore, in the masculinity of man something incomplete. . . . Man, the male, is not truly man except in the heavenly Man, the Son of God."[30]

The mysterious strength of the weaker sex is best shown by the fact that great men who seemed to be totally fearless in other regards feared their wives. In his *Life of Mahatma Gandhi*, Louis Fischer writes, "Gandhi feared neither man nor government, neither prison nor poverty nor death. But he

---

[28] Roy Campbell, unpublished letter to Mary Campbell, May 1924, quoted in Joseph Pearce, *Unafraid of Virginia Woolf: The Friends and Enemies of Roy Campbell* (Wilmington, Del.: ISI Books, 2004), pp. 75–76. (Originally published as *Bloomsbury and Beyond: The Friends and Enemies of Roy Campbell* [London: HarperCollins Publishers, 2001].)

[29] Chesterton, *What's Wrong with the World*, p. 118.

[30] Louis Bouyer, *Woman in the Church* (San Francisco: Ignatius Press, 1979), p. 36.

did fear his wife."[31] This is what Kierkegaard had in mind when he wrote, "Woman is the conscience of man."[32] In his great book *Sexual Suicide*, George Gilder writes, "Women, in fact, possess enormous power over men."[33] We shall discuss later of what this power should consist.

As noted earlier, the fact that the plenitude of a human person should be found in two different but complementary sexes is truly a divine invention. A male saint is best understood by a female one, and vice versa. When a human being is "transformed into Christ," a male saint incarnates all the typical female virtues, such as gentleness, empathy, and compassion, in a male structure. Female saints can manifest a courage and holy audacity that usually are to be found only in men.

These two different but complementary sexes hint at the awesome fact that human beings are, as we have noted, called to collaborate with God in the creation of new human beings, made in His image and likeness. This is an amazing privilege, which is not granted to angels. God placed in Adam's body a living seed capable of fecundating the eggs placed in Eve's body. The role of the father- and mother-to-be is to hope that semen and

---

[31] Louis Fischer, *The Life of Mahatma Gandhi* (New York: Harper and Brothers, 1950), p. 159.

[32] Kierkegaard, *Either/Or*, 2:56.

[33] George Gilder, *Sexual Suicide* (New York: Quadrangle, 1973), p. 14.

egg will be united and give rise to a child of God. In traditional formulation, the semen and the egg are "material causes." The marital embrace is an efficient cause, instrumental in bringing about the union of both. Whether fecundation will take place is, however, something totally beyond the control of the spouses. The Old Testament makes it clear that God alone can give fertility or correct sterility. All that husband and wife can do is to give the new life a chance. They can, however, prevent it. Conscious of this "negative" power, man in his pride can be tempted to take his metaphysical revenge. *The destructive impulse of fallen human nature can arrogantly impede conception for its own selfish purposes.*

This intended collaboration of the married couple and God is highlighted in procreation. The semen and the egg are "pregiven," that is, placed in human beings by God Himself. These material causes are shared through an act of human will. But the soul is created by God alone and is totally "new"; it is not made of a preexisting material. In other words, when the word "*pro-creation*" is used, it clearly indicates that a man, a woman, and God collaborate. Animals reproduce themselves; they copulate. They do not *procreate*. This metaphysical truth is rich in consequences. When husband and wife decide to interfere negatively by artificially preventing the semen from fecundating the egg, or by killing the fecundated egg, they eliminate God's role and refuse to procreate—they merely copulate. They are revolting against their dignity as human persons, who are able to collaborate with God. Artificial birth control simply means eliminating God from the bedroom. Such evil will not end there.

RECEPTIVITY

Receptivity is the seal of creaturehood and the great charisma of women. Aristotle, in spite of his genius, confused receptivity with passivity. This is why he considered the male to be superior to the female. The two concepts are constantly confused and yet are radically different. *Passivity* is clearly indicative of inferiority. A piece of wood, felled by a lumberjack, is purely passive. The woodchopper expresses his will; the wood has none. The woodchopper is in the superior position. The wood has no say about its fate.

A soul opening itself to God's grace, however, is instead clearly *receptive*. The Gospel of Saint Luke sublimely highlights the key importance of receptivity. When the Holy Virgin is asked to be the Theotokos, she speaks the words: *"Let it be done to me."* This is the most perfect expression of receptivity found in the history of the world. The moment Mary spoke these words, the mystery of mysteries took place: God became man in her womb. Perfect human receptivity led to an overwhelming divine creativity—the God-man.

The ever-recurring temptation to place activity over receptivity finds its most powerful expression in Immanuel Kant's epistemology.[34] Knowing, for him, is not to let oneself be fecundated by an object (receptivity) but is, rather, a human interpretation of sensation shaped by the categories of man's human intellect. *Idealism is male epistemology*. It is a tragic derailment of man's relationship to objective reality. Rather than existing independently of his mind, "reality" becomes an intellectual by-product.

That the heart and emotions play a greater role in women than in men is, once again, either an expression of a beautiful female charisma or an indication of how original sin has infected a more universal noble gift meant for men also. The heart is the very center of the person. Let us imagine how strange it would be if a person falling in love should say to the loved one, "I give you my intelligence."

The heart is mentioned some eight hundred times in the Bible. Why is it said that God, in the Old Testament, says to man, "Give me your heart"?[35] The Catholic Church has a feast dedicated to the Sacred Heart. The Bride of Christ has a litany dedicated to the Sacred Heart. In spite of this, many are the Catholic "intellectuals" who refuse to give the heart

---

[34] Epistemology is the study of knowledge. According to Kant, we do not know things as they are but as sensations that are interpreted by the human mind.

[35] Prov 23:26.

the place that the Church gives it in Catholic worship. Granted, the heart can be both the home of evil thoughts and the seed of evil deeds: "For out of the heart come evil thoughts, murder, adultery, fornication, theft, false witness, slander. These are what defile a man; but to eat with unwashed hands does not defile a man."[36] An impure heart engenders impure thoughts and leads to impure actions. Those whose heart is sincere, on the other hand, will hear God's voice: "If you hear his voice today, harden not your hearts."[37]

FRAILTY, THY NAME IS WOMAN

The Liturgy and the Saints in Praise of Womanhood

It is difficult to understand why many women feel so offended when men, particularly many Fathers and doctors of the Church, refer to them as being the "weaker sex." The Liturgy refers to women as the weaker sex: it extols women martyrs because it is admirable that even the weaker sex should show so much courage. Saints Lucy, Eulalia, Agnes, Agatha, Dorothy, Sabina, Perpetua, and Felicity come to mind. The Liturgy sings the praise of these holy women, whose sex was so frail but whose love and courage were so great.

---

[36] Mt 15:19.
[37] Cf. Ps 95:7–8.

A few quotes are in order:

> Thus does our Lord glorify His infinite power, by crushing Satan's head with what is by nature so weak. The enmity put by God between the woman and the serpent, is for ever showing itself in those sublime Acts of the Martyrs, where the rebel angel is defeated by an enemy whom he knew to be weak, and therefore scorned to fear; but that very weakness, which made her victory the grander, made his humiliation the bitterer. Surely, such history must have taught him how powerful an enemy he has in a Christian woman.[38]

Once again, it is the Liturgy that expresses the amazing power that God gives to the weaker sex when they are faithful: "A woman makes sport of the boaster who vaunted he could shake heaven and earth. The roaring lion becomes a startled gnat before the Christian virgin Justina."[39] Before his conversion to Christ, Saint Cyprian wanted, by "charms and spells," to convince the young virgin Justina to yield to the passion of a young man. He consulted the devil, who told him that "no art would be of any service to him against the true dis-

---

[38] Prosper Guéranger, *The Liturgical Year* (Westminster, Md.: Newman Press, 1948–1949), feast of Saint Dorothy (February 6), 4:246.

[39] Cyprian, *Confessio Cypriani Antiocheni* 1.2, quoted in Guéranger, *Liturgical Year*, feast of Saint Cyprian and Saint Justina (September 26), 14:266.

ciples of Christ."⁴⁰ Indeed, faith and love of God cannot be defeated.

Saint John Chrysostom writes:

> I feel an indescribable pleasure in reading the "Acts of the Martyrs"; but when the martyr is a woman, my enthusiasm is doubled. For the frailer the instrument, the greater is the grace, the brighter the trophy, the grander the victory; and this, not because of her weakness, but because the devil is conquered by her, by whom he once conquered us. He conquered by a woman, and now a woman conquers him. She that was once his weapon, is now his destroyer, brave and invincible.⁴¹

When women, conscious of their "fragility," turn to God with both humility and confidence, they are rewarded by receiving the virtue of true courage. The heroic "Little Flower," Saint Thérèse of Lisieux, writes in her autobiography, "I am . . . *weakness* itself."⁴² When animated by love, women have a courage that should put some men to shame. They are truly invincible. This was already recognized in the pagan world, as when, for example, Alcestis sacrificed her life for her husband. The great Dutch poet

---

⁴⁰ Guéranger, *Liturgical Year*, 14:266–67.

⁴¹ John Chrysostom, *Homil. de diversis novi Testamenti locis*, quoted in Guéranger, *Liturgical Year*, feast of Saints Perpetua and Felicitas (March 6), 4:310.

⁴² Thérèse of Lisieux, *Story of a Soul: The Autobiography of Saint Thérèse of Lisieux*, trans. John Clarke, 3rd ed. (Washington, D.C.: ICS Publications, 1996), manuscript C, fol. 15r, p. 224.

Vondel writes, "A single woman is stronger than one thousand men."[43]

Any man affected by the "macho complex" would be well advised to meditate on what happened at Gethsemane and Golgotha. The holy women were at the foot of the Cross. In Gethsemane, all the apostles fled. In an act of true collegiality, all of the apostles fled. Saint John came back later, but we do not know how soon. The heroines were all women, and not only the "holy women" but also Pilate's wife, who urged him not to condemn a holy man. How sad that Adam listened to Eve, who was tempting him, whereas Pilate did not listen to his wife when she gave him wise and loving advice. He believed himself to be exonerated by washing his hands! Jewish women openly commiserated with Christ on His way to Calvary. What a contrast between them and the high priests, and the brutal Roman soldiers. These women fully deserve to be honored by the Church.

We are told in Genesis that God established an enmity between the serpent and the woman, not between the evil one and the "stronger sex," the man (*vir*). This is surprising indeed. Why is the weaker sex in the forefront of this apocalyptic warfare? Nevertheless, it is so. Women—if they follow Mary—have a central role to play in the healing of a sphere

---

[43] Joost van den Vondel, *The Liberation of Hugo de Groot*, quoted in *Encyclopedie des citations*, ed. P. Dupré (Paris: Editions de Trevise, 1959), 8217.

so gravely wounded by sin and so clearly confided to them. Eve was defeated. Mary conquered.

In his book *Woman in the Church*, Father Louis Bouyer wrote of a mother abbess who resented that the Church seemed to assume that women were incapable of exercising authority. To this he answered: "She [the Church] knows you to be so gifted in the exercise of this authority that she found it prudent to provide some reins in giving it to you."[44] There is a fundamental difference between *authority* and *influence*. One thing is certain: even when women have no authority, their influence over men and society, for good or for evil, is immense. It would be interesting to examine whether influence, in the long run, is not deeper and more lasting than authority. Authority relates only to actions; influence reaches into the very core of the person.

As a final point on frailty, what is often dismissed as weakness may be something quite different. Men cry much less than women do. Some men even seem incapable of tears. Is this because they view tears as expressions of sentimentality, weakness, hypersensitivity, and self-centeredness, or is it because their hearts have never been watered and are like deserts? One thing is certain: both in the Old and the New Testaments, some of the noblest characters have shed tears. Joseph cried several times when his brothers came down to Egypt to

---

[44] Bouyer, *Woman in the Church*, p. 97.

buy bread. Even though it is not expressly written, we can assume that King David, who wept easily, cried upon realizing the horror of his sins. The beloved Saint Peter shed abundant tears because he had denied the One he loved. These are noble tears, and one feels sorry for men who can shed tears of rage but seem incapable of tears of contrition. Christ cried twice, once upon facing Jerusalem and realizing that its unfaithfulness would inevitably lead to its destruction, and once upon facing the tomb of Lazarus, even while knowing that He would bring him back to life. The divine tears of our Savior should make us shed tears of gratitude, love, repentance, and contrition. Women, who are able to shed such tears with ease, better reflect the divine heart than dryer natures.

The Gift of Weakness: Humility as Teacher

The Liturgy of the Catholic Church is replete with words reminding us of the key role of humility in Christian life: "The more this virtue enables a man to feel his own weakness, the more, likewise, does it show him the power of God, who is ever ready to help them that call upon Him."[45] "The military spirit means, if anything, obeying the weakest and stupidest man. . . . Submission to a weak man is discipline. Submission to a strong man is only ser-

---

[45] Guéranger, *Liturgical Year*, Tenth Sunday after Pentecost, 11:270.

vility."⁴⁶ Humiliations are often a much-needed teacher of humility. Saint Augustine strikingly expresses this in his *Confessions*: "What manner of man is any man for he is but a man? Let them that are strong and mighty—them that have not yet had the happiness of being laid low and cast down—let them laugh at me."⁴⁷

Saint Augustine's genius was certainly fecundated by his humility. He writes, "When I hear my former life brought forward, no matter with what intention it is done, I am not so ungrateful as to be affected thereat; for the more they show up my misery, the more I praise my physician."⁴⁸ The brilliant rhetorician had to acknowledge defeat in the garden in Milan; Augustine admitted that repeated sins had taken control over his will and that the latter, although still responsible, was no longer morally free. He could not undo what he had freely chosen to do. His numerous defeats led, however, to a glorious victory. From that point forward, Augustine would constantly beg God for His grace. "Da quod jubes et jube quod vis"—that is, "Give me your grace first, and then you can command what you will."⁴⁹

Far from being offensive, the term *weaker sex* can be interpreted very positively. It is a blessing to be

---

⁴⁶ Chesterton, *What's Wrong with the World*, p. 128.

⁴⁷ Augustine, *Confessions*, bk. 4, no. 1, passim.

⁴⁸ Augustine, *Contra litteras Petiliani* 3.11, quoted in Guéranger, *Liturgical Year*, feast of Saint Augustine (August 28), 14:101.

⁴⁹ Augustine, *Confessions*, bk. 10, no. 40.

reminded of one's weakness. Whether one is weaker or stronger than someone else is irrelevant. Blessed is the woman, or the man for that matter, who is aware of her, or his, weakness. Self-assurance is the fast road to a fall. Let us hear Plato's words: "For entire ignorance is not so terrible or extreme an evil, and is far from being the greatest of all; too much cleverness and too much learning, accompanied with an ill bringing up, are far more fatal."[50] Men usually "know" more than women do,[51] but if this knowledge is divorced from wisdom, it will lead to their doom. To repeat the words of the chivalrous Chesterton: "Cleverness shall be left for men and wisdom for women."[52] *Sophia* (wisdom) is a feminine word. It is possible to be wise with little or no scholarship. Scholarship without wisdom is the fast road to heresies and intellectual aberrations. A sharp mind can never compensate for a desiccated heart. The lack of high artistic or intellectual creativity of (most) women has one obvious advantage: men, and alas, often bishops or theologians, have been the creators of heresies. On the negative side, once men become famous, many women (who love

---

[50] Plato, *The Laws*, trans. Benjamin Jowett (New York: Cosimo, 2008), no. 819, p. 174.

[51] Richard Lynn showed that men have more general knowledge than women. Richard Lynn and Tatu Vanhanen, *IQ and Global Inequality* (Augusta, Ga.: Washington Summit Publishers, 2006).

[52] Chesterton, *What's Wrong with the World*, p. 156.

to know famous men) will blindly flock to them and become their enthusiastic disciples. Famous men have an irresistible attraction for some women.

It is easier for a woman to acknowledge her weakness than it is for a man to acknowledge his weakness, and this is, no doubt, a great advantage she has over him. Moreover, women, being physically weaker than men, are more conscious of their creaturehood. Creatures are metaphysically so dependent that they are constantly in need of help. The Church teaches that the world would collapse back into nothingness if it were not for the sustaining action of God. How easily the words "Help me, O Lord, lest I perish" come to a woman's lips. A woman who is in labor prays because, in this supreme moment, she experiences—through a striking paradox—both the amazing privilege granted to her and the humbling precariousness of her situation. In giving birth, she faces death, both for herself and for the beloved fruit of her womb. Looking back upon our lives, most of us must acknowledge that the grievous mistakes we have made were caused by self-assurance and an erroneous conviction that "we knew best." Pride precedes a fall. Plato perceived this centuries ago when, referring to a young man's foolishness, he wrote, "[He who] thinks that he has no need of any guide or ruler, but is able himself to be the guide of others, he, I say, is left deserted of God."[53]

---

[53] Plato, *The Laws*, no. 716, p. 89.

How beautiful are the words of Saint Paul, so keenly aware of his weakness: "For when I am weak, then I am strong."[54] But again: "I can do all things in him who strengthens me."[55] It is in this humble acknowledgment that he proclaims the Christian victory par excellence, the possibility of changing every single defeat into a glorious victory through grace. True, women are "only" women, but men are also "only" men; all of us are "only" creatures, that is, helpless beings constantly in need of divine assistance. The wisdom of Plato perceived that any victory that leads to self-assurance will usually lead to a serious defeat down the road. He writes, "Many a victory has been and will be suicidal to the victors."[56] Hitler was crushed in 1945, but alas, we have reasons to fear that he has been *morally* victorious. The moral poison he had spread early in the twentieth century, the legalization of crime, has now infected the nations that defeated him. Crimes we once condemned with horror are now legal and somehow, therefore, perfectly acceptable.

No, wise women will not be offended by being called weak. What *is* offensive, however, is the implicit claim that men are superior, which is definitely unwarranted. Victory is always achieved by individuals, not by one's sex. Saint Thérèse's auto-

---

[54] 2 Cor 12:10.

[55] Phil 4:13.

[56] Plato, *The Laws*, no. 641, p. 24.

biography gives us the best and wisest answer that women should give when told that they are the "weaker sex." While traveling in Italy, she was struck by the fact that she was always being told that women were not to enter certain places; disobedience carried with it the sentence of excommunication. She lamented the fact that women are often held in contempt even though, at Calvary, they showed much more courage than men. But the conclusion she draws reflects her supernatural attitude: Christ allows women to be looked down upon to enable them to partake of His own fate while on earth. He was rejected, spit upon, and insulted; blessed are those who are allowed to share His fate. In heaven, the last will be the first, and women will then receive their reward.[57]

Whether man or woman, the person who never loses sight of his weakness is clearly on the way to victory because he will, "in season and out of season,"[58] beg God for help. In Him, "we can tread upon . . . high places."[59] Weakness is, then, a universal limitation of humanity. A recognition that one needs help is an act not only of humility but also of sanity. Why did the noble and lovable Peter deny Christ a few hours after having solemnly

---

[57] Thérèse of Lisieux, *Story of a Soul*, manuscript A, fol. 66v, p. 140.
[58] 2 Tim 4:2.
[59] Hab 3:19.

declared that he would die for Him? Because he counted on his own strength. His undiagnosed cowardice led him to an action over which he repented for the rest of his life.

Too often, we forget the gravity of intellectual sins such as pride and arrogance. Often, we assume that sins of the heart are the truly grave ones. Kierkegaard sets us straight when he writes, "The sins of passion and of the heart: how much nearer to salvation than the sins of reason."[60] This should not be interpreted to mean that sins of the heart cannot also gravely offend God, but He Himself preferred the passionate soul, either hot or cold, to the nauseatingly lukewarm one.[61] Chesterton writes, "The dangerous criminal is the educated criminal. We say that the most dangerous criminal now is the entirely lawless modern philosopher. Compared to him, burglars and bigamists are essentially moral men; my heart goes out to them."[62] Our very sick world is today facing the fearful problem of "brilliance without wisdom, power without conscience."[63] The combination of pride and power can lead to the destruction of the world, as we too well know.

---

[60] Søren Kierkegaard, *The Journals of Kierkegaard*, trans. Alexander Dru (New York: Harper Torch Books, 1959), p. 215.

[61] Rev 3:15–16.

[62] G. K. Chesterton, *The Man Who Was Thursday* (Mineola, N.Y.: Dover Publications, 2002), p. 52.

[63] Omar N. Bradley (former chief of staff, U.S. Army), speech in Boston (November 10, 1948), quoted in Fischer, *Life of Mahatma Gandhi*, p. 349.

The conclusion is that the greater our awareness of our weakness, the better we are protected against the attacks of the enemy. All those who forget, be it only for a short moment, to put on the protective armor of humility, are heading for a fall. Christ warns, "Apart from me you can do nothing."[64] Therefore, when women are declared to be the weaker sex, we can turn this to our advantage, and thereby become strong in Him.

THE MORAL FIBER OF WOMEN

Pearl Buck emphasizes the moral superiority of women over men. She writes about Asiatic women, "In centuries of such existence, while she compelled herself to devotion and duty, she accumulated an inner strength which cannot be surpassed."[65] In another book, Buck writes, "Where the woman is faithful no evil can befall. The woman is the root and the man the tree. The tree grows only as high as the root is strong."[66] And further: "The strongest thing on earth is a woman. . . . Let us even be glad the enemy are men and not women, for when women conquer then men are lost indeed."[67] Even

---

[64] Jn 15:5.

[65] Pearl S. Buck, *A Bridge for Passing* (New York: John Day Company, 1962), p. 144.

[66] Pearl S. Buck, *Dragon Seed: The Story of China at War* (Kingston, R.I.: Moyer Bell, 1941), p. 95.

[67] Ibid., p. 232.

the pagan world acknowledges the power of women for good or for evil. The Latin poet Publilius Syrus wrote, "A virtuous woman commands her husband by obeying him."[68]

Solzhenitsyn relates that when a revolt broke out in one of the many Soviet gulags in the early fifties, as the Soviet tanks reestablished "order" by ruthlessly killing anyone standing in their path, "women, desperately trying to shield their men from the cold steel, were bayoneted first."[69] They loved.

In her book *Catherine the Great*, Joan Haslip stresses the superiority of Polish women over men. She writes, "He [Stanislaus] was at his happiest with the feminine members of his court, for the women were far cleverer and better educated. Visitors to Poland were always impressed by the obvious superiority of the women and their interest in politics and the arts."[70]

Wilhelm F. Foerster, the great German pedagogue who lived in Paris for many years, similarly writes that French women are usually superior to their husbands.[71] Nietzsche observes that while the woman is

---

[68] "Casta ad virum matrona parendo imperat." Publilius Syrus, *Sententiae*.

[69] Joseph Pearce, *Solzhenitsyn: A Soul in Exile* (Grand Rapids, Mich.: Baker Books, 2001), p. 130.

[70] Joan Haslip, *Catherine the Great: A Biography* (New York: G. P. Putnam's Sons, 1977), p. 170.

[71] Friedrich Wilhem Foerster, *Erlebte Weltgeschichte* (Nürnberg: Glock und Lutz, 1953), p. 444.

much more wicked than the man, she is also better.[72] One is taken by surprise when reading in Louis Fischer's book on Gandhi as he writes, "Moslem women are the real force behind their men."[73] That this should be true in a culture that has the reputation of looking down on women is worth mentioning.

This superiority is mostly a *moral* one, but in a society like ours, dominated by secular ideals and relativism, moral greatness is no longer appreciated. Rather, creativity, inventiveness, performances of all sorts—domains in which men excel—are seen as alone worthy of our admiration. One of the basic tenets of Communism is that a person's worth is measured by his "productivity." In other words, the "untalented," the weak, the old, and the crippled should be eliminated from the paradise of the workers. In an atheistic world, their existence is not justified, and they are just a burden menacing the glorious future that lies ahead of humanity if it is faithful to the dogmas of Marx.

Chaplains of male and female religious orders will tell you that when women aim at holiness, no sacrifice will ever strike them as too great. When it is suggested that they should make an additional penance for some noble cause, they will immediately give

---

[72] Friedrich Nietzsche, *Ecce Homo*, "Warum ich so gute Bücher schreibe" [Why I write such good books], no. 5. This is another example of when Nietzsche writes a statement that contradicts some of his other statements.

[73] Fischer, *Life of Mahatma Gandhi*, p. 397.

their assent. Men, by contrast, are usually reluctant and feel that what is requested by the rule is enough. Chesterton writes that men are usually more pleasure-seeking than women.[74] It is therefore more difficult for them to achieve what Plato calls "victory over pleasure."[75] Female generosity is confirmed by Cardinal Newman:

> From the first we have been more successful from several causes with women than men; that is a sufficient reason for turning the work of the Oratory in that direction. It is this consideration which has induced me in my visit to Rome to gain from the Holy See an express encouragement of pious women who are disposed to co-operate in our missionary labours. The large sums bestowed upon our Oratory have come nearly entirely from women. The schools, our sick, our poor, our popular music, owe a special debt to the services of women in various ranks of life.[76]

Chesterton has, once again, shared with us a valuable insight: a woman has the tendency—a noble one that can easily derail—of giving her all to what she is doing. He saw that "there must be in every

---

[74] "Women are at once more conscientious and more impatient, while men are at once more quiescent and more greedy for pleasure" (Chesterton, *What's Wrong with the World*, 189). However, Nietzsche writes, "The woman is much more sensual than the man" (*Unschuld des Werdens*).

[75] Plato, *The Laws*, no. 840, p. 191.

[76] Quoted in Placid Murray, O.S.B., *Newman the Oratorian* (Herefordshire, U.K.: Gracewing, 2004), p. 311.

center of humanity one human being upon a larger plan; one who does not 'give her best,' but gives her all."[77] Whether male or female, we are very weak creatures. Truth should never incense us.

---

[77] Chesterton, *What's Wrong with the World*, p. 158.

CHAPTER 4
With Mary: From Defeat to Victory

MARY AS EXEMPLAR: *STELLA MATUTINA* (THE MORNING STAR)

Roman Catholics have no excuse for falling into aberrations because, together with the Orthodox Church, they are blessed beyond measure by their devotion (*hyperdulia*) to Mary, the sweet Theotokos. In contemplating her, in loving her, in meditating on her beauty, they can find all the answers to the grave problems plaguing our society. She is the Mother par excellence. She alone deserves to be the role model of women. She is the Queen of Angels. She is virgin, spouse, mother, and widow. Our Mother Mary, even as she sleeps, breathes out more piety than all the wakeful moments of the rest of the sorry world.

How meaningful that the great male saints have loved her so tenderly. Let us quote a few words taken from Saint Bernard: "Following her, thou strayest not; invoking her, thou despairest not;

thinking of her, thou wanderest not; upheld by her, thou fallest not; shielded by her, thou fearest not; guided by her, thou growest not weary; favoured by her, thou reachest the goal. And thus doth thou experience in thyself how good is that saying: And the Virgin's name was Mary."[1]

Mary, after her divine Son, is the key figure in the Gospels, but it is deeply significant that she speaks only six times, whereas Saint Peter speaks twenty-seven times. Mystery always implies veiling, and the blessed one is teaching women that to be center stage is not their calling. Their mission is best accomplished by "the apostolate of being."

Do I mean that women should remain imprisoned in what the Germans call the three "K"s: *Kirche*, *Kuche*, and *Kindern* (Church, kitchen, and children)? Far from it. "The woman's part is to prepare man himself, and make him the food of God."[2] "Has the woman, then, no power? She has power, and a great power: she must address herself to her husband's heart, and gain all by love."[3]

There is a Catholic answer to this dilemma of what seems to be an insurmountable tension between the

---

[1] Lessons of the second nocturn of the feast, *ex Bernard. homil. 2 super Missus est*, quoted in Prosper Guéranger, *The Liturgical Year* (Westminster, Md.: Newman Press, 1948–1949), 14:172.

[2] Guéranger, *Liturgical Year*, Wednesday within the Octave of Corpus Christi, 10:384.

[3] Ibid., feast of the Sacred Heart of Jesus, 10:422.

woman's veiled status and her high moral calling. It is what spiritual directors call *thema Christi*, the theme of Christ. What does Christ want me to do at this particular moment, on this particular day? This is highly individual, and to understand the divine message calls for a saintly flexibility. A young woman with young children is in a very different situation from a woman who, although married, has not been blessed with children. There are husbands who, because of some handicaps, cannot hold a regular job but who are very good at doing housework. There are women who have a special talent that can glorify God. Each situation is individual, but nevertheless, all of them have one common basis—what is Christ's calling for me *now*?

Holiness always responds to the call of the moment and therefore calls for holy flexibility. This is powerfully expressed in the Rule of Saint Benedict. He writes that as soon as a monk receives an order from his superior, whatever the importance of the task in which he was involved, he should immediately—without a second's delay—abandon the most cherished task to follow God's command. This is truly a holy flexibility; all of us know how hard it is to interrupt a work we are performing. We would only need five more minutes to complete it and yet must, "against nature," leave a word half-written.

This is precisely what the Little Flower did when called upon to perform a task. The same idea is admirably etched in book 8 of Saint Francis de Sales' *Treatise on the Love of God*. Each particular vocation calls for the practice of some particular virtue. A Carthusian practically speaks only to God. A Dominican is called upon to preach. A person called to the holy sacrament of matrimony finds himself in a very different situation from someone who has taken a vow of chastity. A Franciscan friar lives in complete poverty; a father of a family has a duty to provide for the needs of those confided to his care. But one of the mysteries of Catholic life is that if one lives as perfectly as possible one's particular vocation, it potentially will include virtues that are prominent in another vocation. This is why we see saints who have lived in the married state, such as Saint Bridget of Sweden and Saint Francis Borgia, join religious orders upon becoming widows or widowers and make admirable monks and nuns. These two examples could be multiplied.

MOTHER MOST PURE

We have seen in chapter 1 that the Old Testament has clearly indicated that the intimate sphere is a "sore point" where the evil one easily finds access. In order for the virtue of purity to be fully both perceived and realized, we must turn to the New Testament, to Mary, the one who is full of grace and is the most perfect creature of God's work. It is she whose beauty is explicitly referred to by Saint

John in his Apocalypse—a woman "clothed with the sun, with the moon under her feet, and on her head a crown of twelve stars."[4] It is in her that we shall find the dazzling beauty of purity, and it is through her that the putrid wound that has infected the intimate sphere since original sin can be healed. We need meditate only for a moment on the degree of purity that this most beautiful flower of Judaism had to possess in order to become a worthy temple for the second Person of the Holy Trinity. She is totally transparent to God, luminous, and of dazzling beauty. Her womb was to be a sacred cradle in which He could rest for nine months. The dazzling radiance of this feminine place—the tabernacle of the God-man—must have blinded the angels, bringing them "to their knees." Anyone meditating on the role of this womb, mentioned millions of times by those who pray the Hail Mary, will feel sorry for Freud's misguided glorification of the male organ.

"Ever-closed Gate, opened to none save only God," the prayer exults.[5] For if men are granted a visible organ as a symbol of power and strength, the woman is given a hidden one, a womb, the cradle of a new life, which is hidden by a veil. It is a

---

[4] Rev 12:1.
[5] Blessed Notker, sequence for the Purification of Our Lady, quoted in Guéranger, *Liturgical Year*, Purification of the Blessed Virgin (February 2), 3:497; cf. Ezek 44:2.

long-standing tradition that the veil symbolizes sacredness, belonging to God. Knowing from all eternity that His divine Son would be hidden for nine months in the womb of a woman, God covered this sacred organ with a veil. It is clearly a *hortus conclusus*, a closed garden, belonging to God, the keys of which can be given only with God's permission in the holy sacrament of matrimony. Otherwise, one can truly speak of a desecration.

That feminism should have originated in Protestant countries is to be explained by the fact that they have lost a precious pearl: the devotion to the Mother of the Savior. Sigrid Undset remarks that this terrible loss has the inevitable consequence that women, having lost their privilege of taking Mary as their role model, will inevitably lose the particular dignity of the feminine. They exist for the sake of men.[6] A similar thought is mentioned by John Saward (now Father Saward). He writes, "I suspect that the reason why the Protestant denominations have been so vulnerable to the taunts of feminism is that their religion refuses to acknowledge the unique role of woman, of *the* Woman, of our Lady, in the drama of redemption."[7] It is in

---

[6] A. H. Winsnes, *Sigrid Undset: A Study in Christian Realism* (New York: Sheed and Ward, 1953), p. 167.

[7] John Saward, "Thanks for the Feminine," in *The Enemy Within: Radical Feminism in the Christian Churches*, ed. Christine Kelly (Wicken, Milton Keynes, U.K.: Family Publications, 1992), p. 128.

turning to her that we shall find a holy salve that will heal the festering wound of impurity.

The virtue of purity, today either ignored or trampled upon, is rooted in a trembling reverence before a mystery clearly related to God. It is to live in God's presence. The more one meditates on Mary's holiness and beauty, the better one understands that she is the one who, through her radiant purity, will build a bridge that will bring about a total reconciliation between men and women. The more one contemplates her, the more luminously her purity will reveal itself to us. From the moment of her Immaculate Conception, she lived in the constant presence of God. By offering herself completely to Him, she accepted to humbly collaborate with Him in His redemptive work and proved that total donation to God is so fecundating that her very virginity makes her to be the Mother par excellence: "Son, this is Your Mother." Her chaste heart embraces all creatures; consciousness of this fact drove Saint Bernard, one of her most faithful servants, to compose the Memorare.[8] Mary should be the role model for all

---

[8] The Memorare: "Remember, O most gracious Virgin Mary, that never was it known that anyone who fled to thy protection, implored thy help, or sought thine intercession was left unaided. Inspired by this confidence, I fly unto thee, O Virgin of virgins, my Mother; to thee do I come, before thee I kneel, sinful and sorrowful. O Mother of the Word Incarnate, despise not my petitions, but in thy mercy hear and answer me. Amen."

women, telling them that because they share her nature—the nature of the one who is *gratia plena*—they are called upon to be the guardians of purity. It is by imitating her that they will bring healing to a sphere so disgraced by sin.

It is in contemplating Mary that the glorious virtue of purity radiates in all its beauty. Purity implies that one is living in the joyful consciousness that God sees us. It is living in front of Him, rejoicing that He sees us, and grateful that He sees every single thought that we have, every single wish that arises in our hearts, and every single difficulty that we have in our ascent up the holy mountain. He who lives in this consciousness cannot possibly nurture impure thoughts, let alone commit impure acts. What an abyss yawns between any impure act that necessarily tries to "hide" and takes place in darkness, and the reverent, grateful self-donation of the spouses in front of Him Who has permitted them to give themselves to each other.

To speak adequately about Mary's purity, we would need the tongues of angels. All we can do is stammer a few words while adoring the divine mystery incarnated in her. One can speak of two steps in Mary's purity. The first was her Immaculate Conception: she alone, after Adam's fall, was not tainted by original sin. She alone remained faithful to the graces received and kept growing in holiness. Then came the hour of the Annunciation, the earthshaking moment in history—yet unknown to the world—which the angels watched in silent adoration: the young virgin was asked to become the Mother of the Redeemer. Mary's purity is manifested in the very first words that we are blessed to hear from her mouth: "How can this be, since I do not know man?"[9]

What a chaste way of expressing that she is a virgin, and wishes to remain one, to indicate her total dedication to God. The words we use betray our attitude toward the object to which we refer. In our contemporary world, it is a source of grief to hear young girls using words of a coarseness that, years ago, were used only by drunken soldiers. If they meditated for a few moments on the music flowing out of Mary's mouth, they would understand that this sphere is mysterious and should be approached with a trembling reverence. Any coarse reference to it stains the one who utters it. Even the well-intentioned teachers of chastity on Catholic television should meditate on our Mother's words: how coarse their language is compared to the delicacy of Mary's vocabulary.

When promised by Gabriel that motherhood would not deprive her of the precious jewel of her virginity, she spoke the blessed words: "I am the handmaid of the Lord."[10] Her Yes sealed her purity

---

[9] Lk 1:34 (NAB).
[10] Lk 1:38.

with a divine seal. Once again, human words fail even to hint adequately at the mystery that took place. When, in silent contemplation, one adores the mystery of the Incarnation, one faintly realizes what Mary's purity must have been like when inhabited by God Himself, He Whose splendor is such that the angels cover their faces with their wings while singing "Sanctus." This closeness to God, this awareness that He is there, gives the believer a peace and a joy that the world does not know. Those who live in sin not only are deprived of this peace but must necessarily be torn by conscious or repressed feelings of guilt. In this light, the sacrament of penance, when properly understood, is to be seen as a blessed harbor where the poor soul, harassed by the consciousness of its filth and imperfection, finally can find rest.

ARK OF THE COVENANT: GATE OF HEAVEN

Mary's *purity* is matched only by her *humility*. This humble Jewish girl, a descendent like us of Adam and Eve, a daughter of Abraham and of David, is elevated by God to such a height of holiness that she upsets the ontological hierarchy, so strongly emphasized in pagan philosophy, of the superiority of the immaterial over the material. The first great divide in Catholic theology is the one between Creator and creature. This ontological chasm is of such a nature that it can never be bridged by man, but God, in His infinite love, did do so through the Incarnation. Theology and philosophy inform us that angels, being pure spirits, rank above man, and yet — and this is a metaphysical tsunami — Mary is placed above the angels, for she is their queen, *regina angelorum*. As Saint Augustine points out, Christ became *man*, not an angel. All creatures, including angels, must bow in front of Mary's Son and adore Him. Mary, being His Mother, is placed above all angelic beings, above all the saints, and is honored by *dulia* (veneration) — or, more precisely, she alone is entitled to the cult of *hyperdulia*.

The Incarnation — this divine tsunami — is the one event in history that "has made all things new."[11] It has bridged the chasms between man and God, and man and woman, created by original sin. On the one hand, we have a virgin, the most perfect realization of femininity, its perfect *idea* as found in the Creator's mind, united to the God-man — God, who has accepted to become fully man. For nine months, the union between them was so close, so intimate, that their hearts beat together, they breathed the same breath, they ate the same food. The glorious, and dolorous, moment that He left this blessed womb, their spiritual union continued with the same perfection and intensity. He, the Savior, and she, the co-redemptrix, are forever one.

---

[11] Cf. Rev 21:5.

How profoundly meaningful that Christ has a human Mother and no human father. If the feminists had the wit or honesty to acknowledge this dogma, they would not dare slander the Church by proclaiming she has always seen women as inferior.

The Holy Liturgy illumines again and again the key role that Mary plays in the drama of redemption. Her life was adoration and service. Her service was a form of adoration. Feminists infected by the poison efficiently spread by Simone de Beauvoir, Betty Friedan, and their ilk have been persuaded that their role in the family was low class, inferior, and a major obstacle to the cultivation of their talents, which were bound to die in the bud. Shopping, cooking, washing, diaper changing — these are tasks below the dignity of talented females. Has it ever once occurred to them that the *Queen of Angels'* life in Nazareth was devoted to these humble tasks? Performing them in a spirit of faith, animated by her burning love for her divine Son, each one of them glorified God more than anyone could possibly do as a head of state or by commanding a huge financial corporation. The road to perfection is not to be gauged by the secular "weight" of our activities but by the amount of love with which they are performed. Let us think for a moment of how much God was glorified when the blessed one among women was changing the diapers of the King of the Universe. Great theologians would agree that angels in heaven had reason to envy her task.

SINGULAR VESSEL OF DEVOTION: REVERENCE

We have already noted that the virtue of purity is rooted in a trembling reverence before a mystery clearly related to God, to the amazing fact that in this very sphere God and man collaborate in a unique fashion to bring a new life into existence. The parents become instrumental, hoping to unite the precious seeds they have received from God, Who may infuse in their work a new human soul. Important as are the four cardinal virtues, it is regrettable that reverence has not been mentioned as their anchor, for in fact, all virtues presuppose and rest upon reverence. What is reverence? It is respect for things that, because of their nobility and inner worth, call for awe.

When referring to the greatness enjoyed by Athens in the fifth century B.C., Plato writes, "Reverence was our queen and mistress."[12] Time and again, this noble thinker points to the fact that lack of reverence leads to moral decadence. Once man becomes morally blind, political disaster will inevitably follow. Dietrich von Hildebrand writes that reverence

---

[12] Plato, *The Laws*, trans. Benjamin Jowett (New York: Cosimo, 2008), no. 698, p. 74.

is "the mother of all virtues."[13] Conversely, moral decadence goes hand in hand with irreverence. Man is called upon to give the proper response to objects, people, and situations. Plato tells us we should love what is lovable, hate what is hateful. Therefore, we can be measured according to how we respond to things that have an objective value, whether it be to the things that are above us and above all, the sphere of the sacred, the sphere of mystery, and ultimately God, or whether it be to the lower things of earth. Reverence toward God was traditionally expressed by prostrating oneself on the ground, by kneeling, or by bowing. It is deeply regrettable that the symbolism of these actions has been fled from and has become lost. To call these actions "demeaning" is a typical case of moral blindness. It is not by accident that reverence has decreased accordingly as these actions have become rarer. Chesterton wrote that man does not know how tall he is on his knees. How deeply true. Today, we receive Holy Communion standing; that might be one of the reasons why the feeling of sacredness and of awe in front of holy things has

---

[13] Dietrich von Hildebrand, "The Role of Reverence in Education," in *The New Tower of Babel* (New York: P. J. Kenedy and Sons, 1953), 167; *Liturgy and Personality*, newly revised and edited (Baltimore: Helicon Press, 1960), 36; cf. *Fundamental Moral Attitudes*, trans. Alice M. Jourdain (Freeport: N.Y.: Books for Libraries Press, 1950), 5 ("mother of all moral life").

disappeared. Many young people have no experience of the awe-filled. They have respect neither for the sacred, nor for age, nor for mysteries. Infected by materialism, they are impressed only by what is healthy, strong, and productive. I recall asking three priests whether people ever accuse themselves in the confessional of a lack of reverence. The three—one elderly, one middle-aged, and one in his early thirties—after a few minutes of silence said in unison, "Never."

VIRGIN MOST FAITHFUL: PIETY

The Liturgy refers to women as "the pious sex."[14] It is true that, until the feminist revolution poisoned many women, many more females than males attended Church. It is also true that Eastern European *babushki* (grandmothers) were those who kept the candle of faith burning during the diabolical dark night of atheistic Communism, as stated by Paul Evdokimov.[15] This indicates clearly that the mission—the role—of women is *essentially religious*. Their mission is intimately related to eternity. This is why, when all the works of men will be destroyed by fire,[16] the children that women have conceived, having an

---

[14] Taken from "Common Feasts of the Blessed Virgin Mary."

[15] Paul Evdokimov, *Woman and the Salvation of the World: A Christian Anthropology on the Charisms of Women*, trans. Anthony P. Gythiel (Crestwood, N.Y.: St. Vladimir's Seminary Press, 1994), p. 267.

[16] Cf. 2 Pet 3:10.

immortal soul, will live forever. Only those willfully blind can fail to perceive that the devil has achieved his greatest triumph since the victory in the Garden of Eden by convincing women of their inferiority and waging war on maternity.

Saint Bernard tells us that the devil fears Mary more than he fears God. This statement is at first puzzling, but the *doctor mellifluus* (honey-sweet doctor) explains his claim as follows: The devil is pride incarnate. To be defeated in his plans by a humble virgin, and a woman to boot, is for him more humiliating than to be defeated by God, for he knows God's power and strength. Being the incarnation of pride, being the one who said, "I will not serve," it is humiliation that he dreads most. Yet this is precisely what happened, and the Catholic Liturgy is eloquent in its praise of Mary: "Adonai, Lord God, great and admirable, who hast wrought salvation by the hand of a woman."[17] Once again, Mary's glory is proclaimed, for her Yes was necessary for the miracle of miracles to take place. Her fiat ("Let it be done to me") gave her participation in God's loving power.

In the Liturgy celebrating Mary, we find words taken from the Song of Solomon, referring to her matchless beauty and radiance: "Who is this that looks forth like the dawn, fair as the moon, bright

---

[17] Antiphon for the Magnificat, First Vespers for the Fourth Sunday of September, quoted in Guéranger, *Liturgical Year*, feast of Our Lady of Ransom (September 24), 14:261.

as the sun?" Surprisingly, these words celebrating her beauty are immediately followed by words celebrating her power: "terrible as an army with banners."[18] These glorious words shed additional light on why the devil fears Mary, ever virgin. Her sweetness, her humility, and her joy at serving give her a power unmatched by the angels themselves. The paradox is deeply meaningful. All the sweetness of the blessed one—her femininity and her enchanting beauty—is immediately linked to the power that humility has granted her: "He who is mighty has done great things for me."[19]

SEAT OF WISDOM: REFUTATION OF ALL HERESIES

One of the most amazing pronouncements concerning Mary is that she is the one "refuting all heresies." "Gaude, Maria Virgo! cunctas hæreses sola interemisti in universo mundo" (Rejoice, Virgin Mary! You alone in the entire world have destroyed all heresies).[20] Once again, one is amazed and baffled. Mary was not a theologian. She had no doctorate. She did not study. She is not a doctor of the Church. And yet, in her alone we find a refutation

---

[18] Song 6:10.
[19] Lk 1:49.
[20] Office of the Blessed Virgin, seventh antiphon of Matins, quoted in Guéranger, *Liturgical Year*, feast of Our Lady, Help of Christians (May 24), 8:538n.

of all the innumerable errors that the weak and proud human mind has produced through the centuries. Saint Athanasius refuted Arianism. The great Saint Augustine refuted Manichaeism, Donatism, and Pelagianism. Mary refutes them all.

Man's pride can produce intellectual tares, but the wheat of truth can be produced only through Mary's humble receptivity when exposed to the divine sun. The history of philosophy speaks eloquently about man's remarkable ability to invent new errors or to give a face-lift to old ones. It is often a shortcut to fame. However, whatever truth man perceives comes not *from* him but *through* him. This is why true intellectual greatness is always coupled with humility. In *The Republic*, Plato makes the profound remark that if the love of wisdom is looked down upon, the responsibility lies not in her enemies but rather in those who profess to follow her. He has strong words and refers to many so-called philosophers as "arrant rogues."[21] Man's mind easily falls into errors, but there are errors that, referring to the most crucial questions, are deadly in their poisonous consequences. Plato sees that philosophical aberrations are so grave that the very meaning of human life is thereby threatened. Errors about crucial questions such as God's exis-

---

[21] Plato, *The Republic*, in *The Dialogues of Plato*, trans. B. Jowett, 3rd ed., vol. 3 (Oxford: Clarendon Press, 1892), no. 489, p. 187.

tence, the immortality of the soul, the relationship between man and woman, love, and the family inevitably lead to the doom of a society. If this noble and great thinker were alive today, what would he think of the works of most "great philosophers" for the last three hundred years? Even though *wisdom* is what we so desperately need, philosophy is the branch of human knowledge that is despised and publicly scorned because so many philosophers have betrayed their mission. They love neither truth, which requires submission, nor wisdom, which must be lived. They want to be creative.

Mary, by contrast, is the *Queen of Theologians*. Anyone meditating upon the fact that the God-man, Who declared Himself *to be the Truth* — something that no other religious founder has ever dared to proclaim — was hidden for nine full months in her sacred womb will realize that the union between Mary and Truth is so intimate that her very being is impregnated by the Truth. She is a living refutation of any heresy that emerges or reemerges. She need not preach. She need not argue. Her union with her divine Son is the answer and suffices to refute any religious or philosophical distortions.

COMFORT OF THE AFFLICTED: *MATER DOLOROSA*

One of the great mysteries of our earthly existence is that love, this remnant of the earthly paradise, is intimately bound with suffering. We need not even refer to Christ, Whose infinite love made Him embrace the worst conceivable suffering, but only turn our gaze on His holy Mother. We can assume that when this blessed Flower of Judaism spoke her fiat, she must have had an intuition that this Yes implied a share in her Son's crucifixion. Certainly Simeon told her this truth at the Presentation of Our Lord. Mary followed Jesus in the course of His public life and was clearly aware of the deadly hatred of the Pharisees. She accompanied Him on the way of Calvary and was standing at the foot of the Cross. She is the *mater dolorosa*, the "sorrowful Mother." She is called the Queen of Martyrs because, after her divine Son, she suffered more than any other human being. She who is blessed, not only among women but above all men and above all angels, is the one person who suffered most after Christ. If young girls are tempted to be envious of Mary's privilege, they might be unaware that the one who was most blessed was also the one who, after the Savior, suffered most. "So great, it has been said, was Mary's grief on Calvary, that, had it been divided among all creatures capable of suffering, it would have caused them all to die instantly."[22]

---

[22] Bernardine of Siena, *Pro festivit.* V. M., sermo 13, *De exaltatione B. V. in gloria*, art. 2, c. 2, quoted in Guéranger, *Liturgical Year*, feast of the Seven Dolours of the Blessed Virgin Mary, 14:217.

The Fathers and the doctors of the Church declare that Mary did not undergo the pains of childbirth because, being immaculately conceived, she was not tainted with original sin. It is permissible to claim, however, that when delivering her holy Child, she suffered excruciating *psychological* pain and anguish.

While He was lying in her sacred womb, she could protect Him with her own body. Once born, she knew she was delivering Him to a sinful and cruel world. She also knew intuitively that He would be sacrificed to reconcile man with God. She was giving birth to *The Priest* par excellence—the only Priest who was also Victim—by accepting death, "a death He freely accepted" (Eucharistic Prayer II). This supreme sacrifice alone could bridge the abyss that sin had created between God and His rebellious creatures.

Joy and sorrow are so linked on this earth, that once the Divine child was out of her womb, she had the privilege to look at Him face to face, to smile at Him, to tenderly embrace Him. One could meditate for hours on the loving interchange that took place between *The Mother* par excellence and the child Jesus.

Now her sublime task, envied by the angels, was a new one: to attend to His needs, to nurse Him, to bathe him, to lull Him to sleep—the humble tasks of love which, in the light of eternity, glorify God infinitely more than noisy worldly accomplishments.

We know nothing about the life of the most holy family, but we do know that Joseph, Mary, and the child Jesus were glorifying God by their very existence, by their holiness, by their love. Mary was no "intellectual"; she was serving her husband and the blessed fruit of her womb. Any woman meditating upon this undeniable fact will be given the grace of understanding that the most humble task, done with love, glorifies God infinitely more than the most elaborate treatise on theology.

Feminists look down upon homely tasks as demeaning and feel that such tasks are unworthy of them. Mary teaches us that love and humility are two facets of the same jewel. What matters is not so much what we do but with how much love we do it. Anyone who loves the Blessed Virgin and wishes to imitate her cannot possibly look down upon housework as demeaning: it is meant to be a symphony of love. Whether it is cooking or washing, if it is done as a service to God, it certainly glorifies Him much more than arrogant "business" or intellectual work.

CHAPTER 5
Women and Relationship: Women and Motherhood

The mission that God has confided to women is best expressed in the word *mother*. In Genesis, Eve is called "the mother of all living."[1] Every single woman, whether married or unmarried, is called upon to embody that mission, if only in the sense of giving love without counting its cost, grateful for an all too rare "Thank you," whose very scarcity demonstrates that love and suffering are deeply linked on this earth. To be a mother is to understand that to sacrifice oneself is to follow Christ, Who loved us to the very end, knowing that His disciples would abandon, deny, or betray Him. Scripture refers to motherhood as the peak of generous self-giving: "Can a woman forget her sucking child, that she should have no compassion on the son of her womb? Even these may forget, yet I will not forget you."[2]

---

[1] Gen 3:20.
[2] Is 49:15.

When Solzhenitsyn's mother died (which he learned weeks after the fact), he had to acknowledge that he had been a bad son. He wrote to his first wife, Natalya, "I am left with all the good she did for me and all the bad I did to her."[3] Alas, how many sons should deplore their ingratitude. Blessed is the man whose infancy has been watched over, kindled, and penetrated by the eye of a tender and holy mother. That glance has a magical power over the soul of the child; it beams forth sweetness and life, and, as the sun's rays mature the fruits of the earth and sweeten them by the communication of its own substance, so does the mother deposit the sacred character of love in the soul of the child.[4]

The most beautiful contemporary testimony written about motherhood comes from the pen of the saintly József Cardinal Mindszenty. No doubt his holy mother, a simple peasant woman, was, humanly speaking, his joy and consolation during the terrible

---

[3] Joseph Pearce, *Solzhenitsyn: A Soul in Exile* (Grand Rapids, Mich.: Baker Books, 2001), p. 56.

[4] Both motherhood and fatherhood are admirable callings. As remarked by Father Louis Bouyer, they are very different, but superbly complementary (*Woman in the Church* [San Francisco: Ignatius Press, 1979]). Because of the narrow scope of this work, I cannot go deeply into this topic, my theme being essentially to help women rediscover the greatness of their mission. But my humble song to the beauty of maternity should be duplicated by one dedicated to the nobility of paternity. (Steve Wood of Saint Joseph's Covenant Keepers is doing admirable work in this domain.)

years of his imprisonment by the Communists.[5] In the course of his captivity, she was rarely permitted to visit her son. They were never left alone for a single moment (obviously this would have endangered the security of the Communist state), and they were prohibited from speaking about anything except family matters. They could remain together for only a very short period of time. Neither the long distance nor rain nor sleet could deter this elderly woman from giving her child the comfort that she alone could give him. "My mother was the light of the sun for me," he wrote.[6] Elsewhere, in a book entitled *The Mother*, his gratitude and love find moving expressions:

> *The Greatest Vocation.* If I would explain this short word [mother], then I must listen to reason as well as to my heart. Wonderful calling, sharing the power of God in giving life. To be a mother, according to Lovich Ilona, means to accept a child from the hand of God. To be a mother means to give life, to become a servant to the weak and small baby. To be a mother means to comfort and help.
>
> Motherhood is a call to love and service. She is ever giving service. During her girlhood she prepares her soul for this sacred service. She is the servant, when she, like the handmaid of the Lord, carries life in her bosom, when she gives birth to it,

---

[5] Cardinal Mindszenty was imprisoned from 1948 to 1956.

[6] József Mindszenty, *Memoirs*, trans. Richard and Clara Winston (New York: Macmillan, 1974), p. 226.

and gives service from morning to night. She sacrifices her patience, love, health and life. She presses you to her heart—she watches over you. She teaches you to talk, to love and laugh. In the cold of winter, she warms your tiny fingers in her hands. She feeds you milk as an infant and bread when you have grown; in fact, she gives life always. When you lisp "mother" and she answers "My baby", even God must rejoice in His soul.

There are sacrifices which only a mother can make. The happiness of hope and the bitterness of worry only a mother can feel to its utmost depth. The word stands for wonderful steadfastness, forgiving, goodness, inexpressible love and ineffable sacrifices. There is no other dignity which can crown woman with greater dignity than the dignity of motherhood, the greatest gift that a woman could receive. By her motherhood she even outranks man.[7]

The bond between mother and child is so profound that it is no wonder that Chesterton, meditating on it, writes, "No one, staring at that frightful female privilege [to give birth], can quite believe in the equality of the sexes."[8] It is meaningful that the last word most often uttered by soldiers dying on the battlefield is *mother*.

It is high time that women rediscover the beauty and dignity of the home, which should be a place of

---

[7] József Cardinal Mindszenty, *The Mother* (Post Falls, Idaho: Lepanto Press, 2009), p. 55.

[8] G. K. Chesterton, *What's Wrong with the World* (New York: Dodd, Mead and Company, 1912), p. 215.

love, rest, peace, and unity. This is the awesome task of women, who, through the ages, have succeeded in creating a nest where a husband—harassed in the battlefield of professional work—can find comfort and peace. It is the place where children know that they are loved. We all crave to hear, "I am glad that you exist." Alas, I know more than one person who has never heard this sweet music. Unless one discovers that God not only loves one, but has loved one from all eternity, it is inevitable that one will have to fight against despair, and possibly self-hatred.

Motherhood is "God's tenderness"[9] brought down to earth. The massive attack waged on it through contraceptives and abortion threatens to dim the sun in our Western world. One shudders when one reads that Simone de Beauvoir says of herself, "Babies fill me with horror."[10] No word can express the grief that one should feel upon realizing that women, who through the centuries, have given and protected life, now rival men, who from the beginning, along with Cain, have been killers. That millions of girls and women *choose* to murder the fruit of their wombs is the death knell of our society. One can only pray that many of them "know not what they do."[11] In a state of panic and despair

---

[9] Gertrud von le Fort, *The Eternal Woman* (Milwaukee: Bruce Publishing Co., 1954).

[10] Deidre Bair, *Simone de Beauvoir* (New York: Summit Books, 1990), p. 170.

[11] Lk 23:34.

because they have been betrayed and abandoned, they are easily convinced that abortion is a harmless procedure, safe and without consequence, because they have been taught in school that what is within them is only a blob of tissue. Yet anyone who has dealt with women who have collaborated in the murders of their children knows that these women are wounded for life. God's grace can work miracles, but the scar is there.

That the Western world—rotted by comfort and wealth—is dying because of these murderous practices is a punishment, for every sin brings about its own punishment.[12] Much worse is the eternal punishment that awaits those who profit from these crimes against life and God, who die without having shed blood-tears. Abortion is Satan's greatest victory since original sin.

Women play such a crucial role in both society and the Church that the wily devil is now waging a fierce war on femininity and particularly on the greatness of motherhood. He is the mastermind behind the philosophy of feminism. This philosophy selects maternity as its main target, convincing modern Eves that it is the one great obstacle preventing women from developing their talents and reaching "transcendence" and "self-fulfillment."

---

[12] Cf. Augustine, *Confessions*, bk. 1, no. 19.

VIRGINITY: THE PERFECT FORM OF MOTHERHOOD

A consecrated virgin seems to be renouncing motherhood. The very opposite is true. Through her total donation to Christ, she elevates motherhood to a supernatural level, providing it a degree of perfection impossible without the revelation of the New Testament. In a way, one could say that a consecrated virgin says in her heart: My holy hunger for motherhood is such that even many children of my own flesh could never satisfy it. I want, through Christ's love, to open my heart to the whole world, to all those little ones, abandoned, unloved, and rejected. Through Christ, the narrow human heart receives a new dimension, inconceivable on a purely natural level. One of the multitude of glorious achievements of Catholicism and Orthodoxy is to have highlighted the fecundity of virginity. Starting with the Holy Virgin, virgo *prius ac posterius* (virgin before and after),[13] who is the Mother of all of us, the Church has given birth to innumerable young girls who have consecrated their virginity to Him, their holy Spouse. Saint Clare, Saint Catherine of Siena, Saint Teresa of Avila, Saint Thérèse of Lisieux, and Blessed Teresa of Calcutta come to mind. They were virgins, spouses of God, and mothers of innumerable children.

---

[13] From the hymn *Alma redemptoris mater*.

When speaking about the beauty of virginal betrothal with Christ, Saint Ambrose was so eloquent that many mothers prevented their daughters from attending his homilies out of fear that their matrimonial plans would be shattered![14] He tells us, "Virginity has brought from heaven that which it may imitate on earth. And not unfittingly has she sought her manner of life from heaven, who has found for herself a Spouse in heaven. She, passing beyond the clouds, air, angels, and stars, has found the Word of God in the very bosom of the Father, and has drawn Him into herself with her whole heart. For who having found so great a Good would forsake it?"[15]

Blessed Teresa of Calcutta was a virgin whose "fecundity" was such that it would be difficult to count the number of her children and now grandchildren. Being a virgin, she could speak eloquently about this sacred female privilege.

Unmarried women should have spiritual children. Married couples who carry the cross of being childless similarly have no excuse for not having

---

[14] Prosper Guéranger, *The Liturgical Year* (Westminster, Md.: Newman Press, 1948–1949), feast of Saint Ambrose (December 7), 1:364.

[15] Ambrose, *On Virginity,* in *A Select Library of Nicene and Post-Nicene Fathers of the Christian Church*, ed. Philip Schaff and Henry Wace, 2nd ser., vol. 10, *Saint Ambrose: Select Works and Letters* (New York: Christian Literature Company, 1896), bk. 1, chap. 3, no. 11.

"children," either spiritual or adopted, who thrive on their love and dedication.

The Church places consecrated virginity above marriage, even though, through the holy paradox, the latter is a sacrament and the former is not.[16] We should keep in mind that the whole universe is a hierarchy, and to place one value above another (e.g., charity above honesty) in no way indicates a lack of appreciation for the lower one. To claim that Beethoven was a greater composer than Debussy in no way denies the artistic talent of the latter. In the same way, the glorious value of consecrated virginity does not detract from the more common but beautiful value of natural motherhood.

It is worth noting that in both the breviary and the missal, when the feast of a male saint is celebrated, he is listed as an apostle, an evangelist, a martyr (or not a martyr), a confessor, a pope, a bishop, or an abbot. No mention is made of his being celibate or not. When a female saint is honored, by contrast, it is always explicitly mentioned whether or not she was a virgin, in addition to her other attributes. This "nuance" indicates that there is a special link between virginity and women. Mother Church seems to be telling us that there is some subtle distinction between celibacy and virginity by this

---

[16] This preference has led a distinguished Jewish theologian, Michael Wyschogrod, to claim that the Catholic Church has a "distaste" for the sexual sphere. See my article in the *Wanderer*, May 2008.

107

discreet reference to the mystery of the female body. Holy Church communicates so many profound messages, many of which we do not take the time to meditate upon but which are so enriching when, in silence, we contemplate them.

As I mentioned in *The Privilege of Being a Woman*,[17] feminism has had a disastrous effect on marriage, on the family, on society at large, and last, but not least, in the Holy Catholic Church. If women had not been meant to play a crucial role in the Church, their betrayal would not have been so catastrophic. It is precisely because they play a supernatural and essential role that their defection en masse from their nature and role as women has been so wounding.

SAINTLY FAMILY RELATIONSHIPS

Holy Spouses

Particularly enlightening and uplifting is the love that can exist between saintly spouses. The chaste tenderness that can and should exist in Catholic marriage is admirably etched in the life of Saint Elizabeth of Hungary. On her way to holiness from the time she was a little girl brought to Germany from her native Hungary in a silver cradle, she was engaged to Louis of Thuringia. At a very young age, she was very conscious of the dangers to which her beloved fiancé was exposed. As related by Mont-

---

[17] Alice von Hildebrand, *The Privilege of Being a Woman* (Ave Maria, Fla.: Sapientia Press, 2005).

alembert, she shed tears when, playing in the courtyard of the palace, she noticed that a woman of remarkable beauty was being brought into his chambers. She immediately sensed that he was being tempted to sin. When asked the reasons of her tears, she answered, "Because they wish to take my brother's precious soul and destroy it."[18] In fact, the chaste young prince, immediately realizing why that girl was being brought to him, chided the unworthy "chevalier" who had initiated this plan and told him to take the girl back to her family, menacing him with hanging if anything happened to her. Upon seeing the girl leave, sweet Elizabeth dried her tears.

She married young, as was the custom of the time, and gave her husband four children, the fourth one being born shortly after Louis' death during the Crusades. Elizabeth used to get up during the night and spend hours praying in front of their bed. While speaking to God, she would hold the hand of her beloved husband to include him in this holy converse. One likes to picture the tenderness that Louis and Elizabeth felt for each other. Grace had healed wounded nature; love had conquered lust. Generous self-giving had eliminated selfish seeking.

When she heard of her beloved husband's death, Elizabeth's grief was overwhelming. Treated outrageously by her brother-in-law, who wished to capture

---

[18] Charles Forbes Montalembert, *The Life of Saint Elizabeth of Hungary* (Charleston, S.C.: BiblioLife, 2009), p. 134.

the throne, she was actually thrown out on the streets, where she lived in abject poverty with her little children. She, who had helped so many poor, found no one to succor her in her distress. She turned to God, carried His Cross, and died at the age of twenty-four. She and one of her daughters, Saint Gertrude, were canonized. Once again, we witness how the grace of the sacrament of matrimony can restore the pristine beauty of the intimate sphere. Grace abounds where sin could easily triumph.

The holiness of the Church is eloquently proved by the fact that those who feed themselves on the sacred food she offers can recover the joy that Adam felt upon seeing Eve. As mentioned in the Liturgy of Good Friday, the sin of our first parents was transformed into a *felix culpa* (happy fault), whose healing opened the door to a beauty still greater than the one first granted to our first parents.

No doubt, the parents of the Little Flower, both of whom had totally given their hearts to God, are another instance of the rebirth that grace and the sacraments can effect in the relationship between man and woman. One cannot help but wish that they may be beatified. Both of them had been drawn to religious life, and even when married, they hesitated to live as husband and wife.[19] But God clearly

---

[19] John Clarke, prologue to *Story of a Soul: The Autobiography of Saint Thérèse of Lisieux*, 3rd ed. (Washington, D.C.: ICS Publications, 1996), p. 2.

had His plans. Their virginity had to be "sacrificed" in order for them to give birth to the Little Flower. Beautiful as virginity is, superior as it may abstractly be to marriage, what matters above all is one's love for God.

Mothers and Sons
Saint Augustine

Saint Augustine lived a life of sin until his conversion at the age of thirty-three, when he was baptized by Saint Ambrose. He then decided to consecrate his life to God. Responding to God's grace, he no longer wanted to have children of his flesh. He opted for the spiritual fatherhood that is much more fecund than the physical. The son of his early sin, Adeodatus, whose extraordinary intelligence awed his father, died after Augustine's mother, Monica.

The reward that God gives to those who ardently wish to follow Him was soon granted to mother and son. While waiting in Ostia for the ship that was to take them back to their homeland, Monica, the model of mothers, and Augustine, the prodigal son, shared *together* a mystical experience in which, for a short moment, they tasted the sweetness of eternity. Augustine has etched this in his own inimitable style.[20] As far as I know, it is the

---

[20] Augustine, *Confessions*, bk. 9, nos. 23–26.

only case in the history of Christianity in which a man and a woman share the same overwhelming experience of closeness to God. It is deeply meaningful that it should take place simultaneously in a woman (a mother fully worthy of this name) and a man (a son) whose mother had given him birth twice. He writes, "For out of her life and mine one life had been made."[21]

The rupture between male and female was healed through grace. Let us recall that the young Augustine had paid scant attention to the warnings of his holy mother. After all, she was "only a woman."[22] Now he knew better. Even though as a young man he was definitely affected by the "macho complex," Monica's holiness made a deep impression upon him. As she lay dying, she told him that "she had never heard [him] speak a harsh or disrespectful word to her."[23] He looked down upon women, but her holiness *forced* him to pay her the respect and love that she deserved. Her *words* made little impression upon him. Her *being* filled him with awe: the powerful and silent message of those who radiate a peace that the world cannot give. Important as the "apostolate of the word" is,

---

[21] *The Confessions of St. Augustine*, trans. John K. Ryan (New York: Doubleday, 1960), bk. 9, no. 30, p. 225.

[22] Cf. ibid., bk. 2, no. 7, p. 68.

[23] Ibid., bk. 9, no. 30, p. 225.

the "apostolate of being" is God's preferred tool to bring sheep into the fold. The first without the second is unlikely to bring fruits.

Other Saints

The sweet union that God meant to exist between mother and son is duplicated again and again in the history of the Catholic Church. Let us think of the tender bonds existing between Saint Bernard and his mother, and between Saint Francis de Sales and his, who was fifteen years old when she gave him birth. Like Saint Augustine, Saint Francis profoundly mourned his mother's death while lovingly accepting God's will. Let us recall the bond between Mamma Margarita and Saint John Bosco. How selflessly she shared his apostolate by living with him, providing for him, and patiently accepting the devastation that "his sons" perpetrated in her vegetable garden while playing their wild boyish games.

The victory achieved by Mary in reconciling man and woman started at the very moment of her Immaculate Conception. Her body was fashioned to be a tabernacle worthy to receive the Savior of the world. Her dazzling purity bears fruits of such sweetness, such that they make the Church exclaim, "Felix culpa!" We shall see that the holy duet—which, thanks to her, can now be sung by man and woman reconciled—will surpass in beauty the song that Adam and Eve sang when they were first given to one another. A fearful defeat is now changed into a glorious victory.

Fathers and Daughters

The luminous tenderness we found between Augustine and Monica has a perfect duplicate in the love found between holy fathers and their holy daughters. In a sick world like ours, in which the word *incest* is, alas, commonplace, it is so uplifting to read the story of the pure and tender bond that can exist and has existed between a father and a daughter.

Saint Thomas More

A "man for all seasons," Thomas More, in his relationship with his daughter Margaret, offers us an example of one of the most moving bonds that can exist between father and daughter. Anyone becoming acquainted with his life will be profoundly inspired to meet a layman who is a lawyer, a great humanist, a married man (married twice, in fact), a father of four children, and a man whose career brought him to the pinnacle of human greatness. He rose to be the chancellor of England, the second most important position in the government.

Attracted by Carthusian spirituality when he lived as a young man close to one of their monasteries, he daily partook of their prayer life, but he realized that in spite of his wishes God was not calling him on this straight path to holiness. He was called, rather, to reach holiness as a layman, saying wisely that he preferred to be a pure married man than an impure monk.[24] Laypeople too should hear the call of Christ, *Sequere me* ("Follow me"—words spoken by Jesus to His disciples).[25] Thomas More took this very seriously. He always wore a hair shirt (it was the privilege of Margaret, his daughter, to wash it) and lovingly taught his children the true faith.

His first wife died at the age of twenty-three, leaving him with four young children. He obtained permission to remarry within a month of her burial, as he needed a mother to take care of his little ones. Dame Alice was a widow who had had several children, the youngest of whom was still with her. In his professional life, Thomas More went from success to success, but his heart was always longing to be with his beloved family, his first priority after God.

The oldest of his four children, Margaret (followed by Elizabeth, Cecily, and John), had a very special relationship with her father. He wanted his children to study Latin and Greek, and Margaret's accomplishments were so remarkable that she earned the amazement of experts.[26] More important, there was a special affinity between father and

---

[24] Daniel Sargent, *Thomas More* (New York: Sheed and Ward, 1933), p. 31.

[25] E.g., Lk 5:27; 18:22.

[26] James Monti, *The King's Good Servant but God's First: The Life and Writings of St. Thomas More* (San Francisco: Ignatius Press, 1997), 63, p. 216.

daughter—that type of mysterious understanding that can often dispense with words. A glance often suffices. We are blessed by having some of their letters to each other. They give us precious insights into the beauty of a friendship rooted in Christ while having all the tenderness that close family ties give.

But as human life is a vale of tears, Thomas More tasted the bitterness of disappointment when Margaret married William Roper in 1521. The young man had caught the subtle bacteria of Lutheranism, and this caused his father-in-law deep sorrow. In a letter to Margaret, Thomas More tells us that, in spite of all his efforts, he had not succeeded in opening William's eyes and could do nothing more than confide him to God.[27] It clearly was the right move. Later, the young man returned to the one true faith. One can imagine the cross that this was for Thomas More, whose attachment to the Holy Catholic Church cost him his life.

The situation in More's England would have been run of the mill had it not cost so many souls. England's king at that time, Henry VIII, had at first staunchly opposed Luther and was given the glorious title of *defensor fidei*. But the devil knew how to tempt him by giving him an adulterous and overpowering attraction for Anne of Boleyn. King Henry had to find, however, a "legal" excuse to annul his twenty-year marriage to Catherine of

---

[27] Ibid., p. 131.

Aragon. He decided that his marriage to Catherine was illegal—Catherine had previously been married to his older brother, although she had not lived with him. (It apparently took the king some twenty years to have an attack of "conscience.") Henry's own marriage to Catherine had been made with a lawful papal dispensation. The pope could not annul Henry and Catherine's legitimate marriage, but Henry would not accept Church authority in the matter. Henry tried to win the British episcopacy to his side, and he had, alas, no great difficulty in winning unheroic bishops to endorse his wishes and proclaim him head of the Church of England — and therefore able to grant the appearance of his own annulment. Only one bishop resisted, preferring to lose his life rather than to betray his faith.

Having secured the religious powers of his kingdom, the king turned to the secular powers. He demanded that Thomas More, who had wisely resigned from the chancellorship, recognize him as Supreme Head of the Church of England. Thomas had to refuse, and he was imprisoned in the fearful Tower of London in April 1534. Enormous pressure was put upon him to change his mind. His reputation as a man of the greatest integrity meant that his endorsement was crucial to the king. In a letter written to his daughter Margaret while he was imprisoned, More signed, "Your tender loving father."[28]

---

[28] Ibid., p. 406.

Margaret, on her side, wrote to him that his heart was "a pleasant palace for the Holy Spirit of God."[29] Facing a horrible death, More found his comfort in meditating on the passion of Christ and told his daughter what her loving letters meant to him during a period when she was prohibited from visiting him.

Alas, for a while his wife, too, tried to persuade him that it was most unreasonable to be lodged in a dirty place, infested by mice, when he had a lovely home, where he would be surrounded by the people he loved. Margaret, too, out of deep love for her beloved father, urged him to take the oath of allegiance to the king. After all, every bishop in the kingdom had done so with the exception of John Fisher, the bishop of Rochester. This must have given Thomas More a taste of the sorrow Christ experienced in Gethsemane when He was abandoned by His disciples in their first true test of collegiality. For a short period, Margaret played the role of Eve, as he plainly told her: she tempted him. But the most tender bonds could not sway this great hero of the faith. To his joy, Margaret opened her eyes and totally accepted his heroic sacrifice and prayed that "he would stand firm in obeying God's will."[30]

Then came the fearful day, July 6, 1535, when Thomas More was to be executed. The king, in his "kindness," ameliorated the form of execution.

---

[29] Ibid., p. 407.
[30] Ibid., p. 414.

Instead of hanging, followed by drawing and quartering, More would only have his head cut off. To which Thomas More dryly commented: "God keep my friends from the pardon of the King."[31]

More, whose face expressed an extraordinary nobility, was endowed with a tremendous sense of humor, which is a modest form of humility. He kept it to the very moment of his death. While lying on the scaffold, he carefully "shove[d] his beard . . . out over the block . . . remarking that it was not to be cut: 'it had never committed treason.'"[32] More ended his life by kissing the executioner. The usual custom was to have the severed head parboiled and the skull exposed. Margaret managed to bribe the executioner and was able to keep the precious relic. When she died, some nine years later, she was buried holding this treasure in her arms.[33] Now they are united in heaven and give the world a sublime example of the beauty of a father-daughter relationship in Christ.

Saint Teresa of Avila

Several times in her autobiography, Santa Teresa of Avila describes the profound bond that united her with her father. When she realized that she was called to religious life and informed her father of her vocation, he was so distressed that he begged

---

[31] Ibid., p. 297.

[32] Sargent, *Thomas More*, p. 299.

[33] Monti, *King's Good Servant*, p. 451.

her to postpone entering a convent until his death. She writes, "Era tanto lo que me queria" (His love for me was so great).[34]

She asked friends to try to persuade him to accept this cross, without any success. Teresa decided to "escape" anyway, and early one morning, accompanied by her brother Antonio, whom she had convinced to enter a monastery, she left the paternal home. Her grief was such, however, that she writes: "No creo sera mas el sentimiento cuando me muera" (I could not conceive that dying was worse).[35] She knew that she was doing God's will at the cost of breaking her father's heart. It was the story of Abraham in reverse.

Soon afterward, when she was forced to leave the convent because her health had broken down, her father once again showed his tender love for her: "Era grande la diligencia que traia mi padre para buscar remedio" (My father showed great diligence in looking for a cure [for me]).[36]

After unbelievable physical trials, she went back to her convent, where her father visited her regularly, and she convinced him to practice mental prayer. She was guiding him on the way to holiness, and he made rapid progress. For a while, she herself stopped this

---

[34] Teresa of Jesus, *Obras Completa* (Madrid: Biblioteca de Autores Cristianos, 1982), chap. 3.

[35] Ibid., chap. 4.

[36] Ibid.

holy practice, using her miserable state of health as an excuse. But one day she recognized how dangerous this was for her soul; courageously overcoming her sufferings, she began anew and remained faithful to the very end of her life to the practice of mental prayer. In her autobiography, she describes admirably her ascension of the holy mountain.

Her closeness to her father continued until his death. She was permitted to assist him during the last days of his life and proved herself to be the most loving and talented nurse, even though she was herself ailing. She dedicated herself totally to alleviating his sufferings, trying to pay back all the love and attention he had given her previously. When her father was crushed by unbearable back pains, she told him that he was partaking in Christ's pains while carrying his cross. From this moment on, he never again mentioned his agony. In her deep attachment to her father—"como yo queria tanto a mi padre" (as I loved my father so much)[37]— Teresa also suffered much. His last hours were edifying. He expressed his regret not to have spent his whole life in a penitential order and longed for eternity. Teresa had the consolation of being present at his holy death. The union between them was so profound because their deep affinity and their

---

[37] Ibid., chap. 7.

reciprocal affection was rooted in Christ, *fornax ardens caritatis* (burning furnace of charity).

Saint Thérèse of Lisieux

Equally moving is the love between Saint Thérèse of Lisieux and her father. Although he was no longer young when she was born (he was fifty), their mutual love gives the lie to the common notion that there can be little understanding between those separated by too great an "age gap." She tells us that she was the most cherished child in her family, perhaps because she was the youngest. Several times in her autobiography, *Story of a Soul*, she expresses the tenderness of her devotion for her father and how "proud" she was of him because of his nobility and deep piety.

When fifteen, Thérèse felt that Christ was calling her to become a Carmelite, following in the footsteps of her sisters Marie and Pauline. Her love for Christ was such that nothing could shake her conviction that she had a religious vocation, but she knew that to follow the calling of her Beloved implied the heartbreaking sacrifice of saying good-bye to her father. The sweet intimacy that had reigned between them would have to be sacrificed and put on the altar. She chose Pentecost Sunday to speak to him. She found him in the garden, contemplating nature. Tears welled in her eyes. He gently asked her the cause of her pain. She told him that she was asking him for permission to enter the convent at the age of fifteen. Anyone reading this book should pick up her autobiography and read the sublime beauty of her holy father's fiat. The moment he sensed that God was asking him to make this supreme sacrifice, he said yes, without a moment's hesitation.

Story of a Soul makes many allusions to the depth of the bond that existed between father and daughter—an existential proof that, through the Incarnation and the Theotokos, the admirable complementarity that God had intended between man and woman was now totally reestablished. More than that, it received a luster that was probably not possible in Eden because the Incarnation had not yet taken place.

We must again marvel at the fact that such a sublime bond can exist between a man and a woman. Far be it from us to exclude the possibility that beautiful bonds can exist between father and son and mother and daughter. The Roman Catholic Church—in whose hands are the healing keys of the chasm separating man and woman—has shown us repeatedly through her history that between the two sexes there is a complementarity that cannot be duplicated in people of the same sex, however deep their bond may be.

Holy Siblings

It is too little known that the great Saint Ambrose, who played a crucial role in Saint Augustine's conversion, had a most tender love for his sister, Marcellina. At an early age, she had consecrated her virginity to

God and "was heart and soul in all the great undertakings of her brother the bishop."[38]

That their pure and ardent affection was reciprocal is expressed in one of his letters to her: "To my sister Marcellina, dearer to me than mine own eyes and life."[39] These are strong words that prove that an overwhelming love of Christ can transform the weak human heart and can give it a pure ardor and an ardent purity. There is something particularly beautiful when the natural bonds of blood are transfigured by supernatural love. This is, once again, one of the miracles of grace.

A better-known sublime friendship is to be found between the "holy twins" Saint Benedict and his sister, Saint Scholastica. The closeness and tenderness of their union is movingly related in Saint Gregory the Great's *Life of Saint Benedict*:

> [Benedict's] sister Scholastica, who was consecrated to God from her very childhood, used to come once a year to see him; unto whom the man of God was wont to go to a house not far from the gate, within the possession of the monastery. Thither she came one day according to custom, and her venerable brother likewise with his disciples; where, after they had spent the whole day in the praise of God and pious discourses, the night drawing on, they took their refection together. As

---

[38] Guéranger, *Liturgical Year*, feast of Saint Ambrose (December 7), 1:362.

[39] Ibid.

they were yet sitting at table, and protracting the time with holy conference, the religious woman, his sister, entreated him saying, "I beseech you, leave me not this night, that we may talk until morning of the joys of the heavenly life." To whom he answered, "What is this you say, sister? By no means can I stay out of my monastery."

At this time the sky was serene, and not a cloud was to be seen in the air. The holy woman, therefore, hearing her brother's refusal, clasped her hands together upon the table, and bowing her head upon them she prayed to Almighty God. As she raised up her head from the table, there began such vehement lightning and thunder, with such abundance of rain, that neither venerable Benedict nor his brethren were able to put foot out of doors. For the holy woman when she leaned her head upon her hands poured forth a flood of tears upon the table, by which she changed the fair weather into foul and rainy.

Then the man of God perceiving that by reason of thunder and lightning with continual showers of rain, he could not possibly return to his monastery, was sad and began to complain, saying, "God Almighty forgive you, sister, what is this you have done?" To whom she made answer, "I prayed you to stay and you would not hear me: I prayed to Almighty God and He heard me. Now, therefore, if you can, go forth to the monastery, and leave me." But he, not able to go forth, was forced to stay against his will. Thus it happened that they spent the night in watching, and received full content in spiritual discourse of heavenly matters.[40]

---

[40] Gregory the Great, *Dialogues* 2.33, in *The Very Rev. Father Paul of Moll: A Flemish Benedictine and Wonderworker of the*

Three days later, Saint Benedict saw his sister's soul leave her body in the form of a dove.[41] The Liturgy has these beautiful words: "Plus potuit, quia plus amavit" (The one who loves more can do more).[42]

HOLY FRIENDSHIPS

The admirable complementarity between man and woman has also brought about the flowering of many holy friendships in the history of the Catholic Church. They are neither the relationships between mother and son, nor between father and daughter, nor between brother and sister, but are the holy affinity existing between mature persons of different sexes.

It is not by accident that great female saints have been under the direction of men. I cannot think of any male saints that have been under the guidance of a woman, but this does not exclude the fact that they can be and have been strongly marked by their spiritual contact with saintly women.

The friendship between male and female saints is a huge topic. We shall limit ourselves to mentioning

---

Nineteenth Century, 1824–1896, by Edward van Speybrouck, 2nd ed. (Clyde, Mo.: Benedictine Convent, 1914), pp. 327–29. (Reprinted in *The Life of Saint Benedict* [Rockford, Ill.: TAN Books and Publishers, 1995], pp. 45–46.)

[41] Gregory the Great, *Dialogues* 2.33, in *Very Rev. Father Paul of Moll*, p. 329.

[42] Antiphon for the feast of Saint Scholastica, in Guéranger, *Liturgical Year*, feast of Saint Scholastica (February 10), 4:270.

some of the most prominent examples, selecting three pairs who are particularly moving in their chaste ardor.

It is too little known that a saintly woman, Paula, and her daughter Eustochium, spiritual daughters of Saint Jerome, moved to Bethlehem and encouraged the saintly scholar to complete his famous translation of the Bible, the Vulgate. Attacked from all sides, he wrote these spiritual daughters: "Handmaids of Christ, shield me with the buckler of your prayers from those who malign me."[43] When discouraged by the constant attacks leveled at him, he knew he could count on the devotedness and affection of these two women. Very feminine, they stayed in the background, but their knowledge of the Bible and of Latin was no doubt a powerful incentive for Jerome to proceed in his labor of love.

When Paula died, reciting the verses "I have chosen to be an abjection in the house of my God, rather than to dwell in the tabernacles of sinners," Jerome was so profoundly affected that he, too, seemed near his end.[44] It is easy to imagine how those whose particular satisfaction is to detect sexual evil could interpret this profound grief as some sort of repressed sexuality. Only pure eyes will be able to see God or understand this type of sorrow.

---

[43] Jerome, *Præf. in Reg.*, quoted in Guéranger, *Liturgical Year*, feast of Saint Jerome (September 30), 14:288.

[44] Ps 84:10; Guéranger, *Liturgical Year*, 14:289–90.

Saint Jerome felt that he had to "excuse" himself "for giving one half of the human race a preference over the other."[45] Likewise, when Saint Francis de Sales wrote to Philothea, he also was criticized for addressing himself to women: *philothea* refers to a female lover of God. He shielded himself from attacks by writing his *Treatise on the Love of God*! But Jerome defended himself by saying, "I know that some find fault with me for writing to women; let me say, then, to these detractors: If men questioned me on the Scripture, they should receive my answers."[46] In other words, he would have given men as much attention if only they had requested it. Men are grateful when they are questioned and challenged to develop their talents. Once again, we see that a woman's receptivity is a great gift both for herself and for the complementary sex. A reverent questioning, no doubt, was a form of inspiration to Jerome.

A second, more famous, example of holy friendship occurs between Saint Francis of Assisi and Saint Clare. When Clare, a young, beautiful, and noble girl, coming from of one of the most prominent families in Assisi, heard Francis speak in San Rufino, and then in San Giorgio, she knew that she was called to follow in his footsteps. When a female heart is inflamed by love, no obstacle is viewed as

---

[45] Guéranger, *Liturgical Year*, 14:289.

[46] Jerome, *Ep.* 65 *al.* 140 *ad Principiam*, quoted in ibid.

too great. Clare's pious Catholic parents thought that there could be too much religion and, having made matrimonial plans for her, were deeply upset when the young girl declared that she would not take a human husband. She actually needed the help of the Franciscan friars to escape from her house during the night and to find her refuge in a convent. How shocking from the "outside"; how sublime from the "inside." To have young men help a young girl to leave her paternal home in the darkness of the night certainly did not bode well or look respectable, but this was all for God's glory. Saint Francis found refuge for her in San Damiano, where later two of her younger sisters and even her mother, after she became a widow, joined her. She was a woman, and she wept upon leaving her father and mother; Saint Teresa of Avila and the Little Flower also went through the same agony. But Clare's love for Christ was stronger, and this "little plant" of Saint Francis, as she liked to call herself, grew strong under his guidance.

Not much is known about their sublime friendship. But we do know that Saint Francis came often to San Damiano for help and guidance. We also know, as related by Jörgensen,[47] that Saint Francis, fearing that Clare was too attached to him, came less and less frequently. When Clare was informed

---

[47] Johannes Jörgensen, *Saint Francis of Assisi: A Biography*, trans. T. O'Conor Sloane (Longmans, Green, and Co., 1912).

that he was close to death, she asked for permission to pay him a last visit. This consolation was denied, but she was informed that, before her death, both she and the sisters would see him. Saint Francis, as expected, kept his word, and his lifeless body was brought to the little church of San Damiano.

Surprisingly enough, Saint Francis' special friend Jacopa de Settesoli, a Roman lady affectionately called "Brother Jacoba," with whom he also had a beautiful friendship, was allowed, upon hearing that Saint Francis was dying in Portiuncula, to rush to his side and bring him a cake that she knew he loved particularly. The holy freedom of a saint is here doubly expressed: a woman is allowed to come to his bedside, and he eats with pleasure and gratitude a dainty, he who had mistreated Brother Ass—as he nicknamed his body—so badly that at the end of his life, he felt that he had to apologize to him. We are told that when he died, "Weeping she fell upon the master's lifeless body and with burning tears flowing, kissed over and over again the wounds in the feet and hands of the dead saint."[48] Blessed tears, pure tears, holy tears of true spiritual love.

For a third example, consider how the ardor, tenderness, and sublimity of the spiritual friendship finds a particularly beautiful expression in the words that Saint Bernard, the great lover of Mary, writes to his friend the countess Ermengard:

---

[48] Ibid., p. 334.

Why can't I bring my spirit just as much before your eyes as I do this paper, thus showing you the feelings of love in my heart which the Lord pours into me, and the zeal for your soul with which he fills me. Truly, you would recognize that no words, and no pen can express my feelings. I am with you spiritually, though physically separated. It is true I cannot show you my heart since it is impossible for me to entirely reveal it to you, it depends on you to understand it; you need only look into your own to find mine therein, and to ascribe to me as much love for you as you feel for me. . . . You will now understand how you have, since my departure, kept me entirely with you; because for my part, I can truly say that I have not left you when I departed, and that I can find you everywhere wherever I go. . . . My heart is at the pinnacle of joy as soon as I receive news of the peace of your heart. I am happy when I know that you are happy, and in your rest I find mine.[49]

No comments are necessary. Only through grace and the supernatural can this sublimity of holy friendship be reached. It is, however, to be remarked that a holy friendship between a man and a woman, rooted in Christ, does not lose anything of its ardor and tenderness. On the contrary, all the virtues of natural love blossom on sacred ground and exhale a perfume that can come only from above. Concupiscence has been chained by humility and reverence,

---

[49] Quoted in Dietrich von Hildebrand, *Man and Woman: Love and the Meaning of Intimacy* (Chicago: Franciscan Herald Press, 1966), pp. 70–77.

keys to purity and true love. This is possible only because such a love is in Christ. It is a partaking of Christ's love for the beloved, a love that could not have entered a man's head. Not only is supernatural love the fulfillment of what every noble natural love aspires to—in its eternal aspect—but it in no way eliminates the hierarchy between loves. Christ loved His holy Mother more than any other creature. Saint John was Christ's favored disciple. Nevertheless, Christ's love includes all men.

It is this divine quality, and this divine quality alone, that enables saintly loves to have this daring intensity that we find formulated in the words that Blessed Jordan of Saxony addressed to Blessed Diana: "I feel in my own leg the pains which you suffer in yours."[50] These are the words that the blessed one among women must have uttered at the foot of the Cross.

When Saint Jane Frances de Chantal lost her beloved husband, there was fear for her life. She had given him six children, the last one being born just when her husband was accidentally killed by his cousin during a hunting trip. Her despair was such that, in no time, she became a skeleton. Her love for him was so deep that her heart was literally crushed by sorrow. Much grace was needed to give her the courage to realize that being a widow magnified her duty to be a mother, the only parent left

---

[50] Quoted in ibid., p. 76.

to her four fatherless young children. (Two had died soon after their birth.) She had to live for them. With a broken heart, she devoted herself to their education.

We all know that a few years later, she met Saint Francis de Sales. Through his guidance, she became the mother of a great order, the Order of the Visitation. This is one spiritual friendship about which we have much information. We have the letters that the great spiritual guide Saint Francis de Sales wrote to her. After his death, when she was given the task of bringing order to his huge correspondence, she found all the letters she had written him from the time that they met until his death in 1622. Upon reading the comments that the saint had written in the margins of her letters, she did not hesitate to burn them. These remarks contained such a high praise of Saint Jane that she wanted them erased because of her humility. Thank God, we still have his letters to her, which manifest the depth and sublimity of their spiritual love.

What is striking is that this holy friendship started almost immediately after their first meeting in Dijon in 1604. His very first letters to her manifest that, from the very beginning, God had placed a deep affinity between these two holy souls. Their holy friendship could traverse in a very short span of time what usually would take weeks and months of maturation.

He does not hesitate to write, "I am totally yours," indicating very plainly that it is God who has planted this holy inclination in his heart. The spiritual perfume of these writings combines a holy daring with a holy reserve. It is a clear stamp of the supernatural origin of this transfigured love, the sort of love all of us will enjoy in eternity. Further, Saint Jane and Saint Francis soon became aware that in placing this holy ardor in their hearts, God was gently leading them to realize that they were called upon to found together a new holy congregation, the Order of the Visitation.

Their joy of being together was always rooted in a clear consciousness that God was between them. This common *sursum corda* (lifting up of hearts) was exclusively for His glory and had to be sacrificed for the sake of charity. As the order started to develop at an amazing speed, both saints were so taken up by this holy task that for the last three years of Saint Francis de Sales' life, he and Saint Jane corresponded only by letters. Their friendship had to be put on the altar. The last time they met was in Lyon, shortly before Saint Francis' death. Saint Jane had made a long list of the problems with which her soul was struggling. When Saint Francis saw her, he asked her what was on her mind. She informed him that there were many issues related to the foundations that she wished to discuss with him, as well as the state of her own soul. Witnessing her anxiousness to discuss the latter first, Saint Francis de Sales told her gently that he was expecting her to be "all angelic" and that he wished to discuss the problems of the order first. This took so long that no time was left to unveil to her beloved spiritual director her own concerns. But Francis, conscious of her disappointment, told her that he would give his answers in Annecy.

Soon afterward, however, he had a stroke, and he died within a few days. When his body was brought back to Annecy, Saint Jane, while praying next to his casket, received all the answers he had promised his beloved daughter that he would give her. This is how God rewards heroic obedience.

When the process of beatification was in progress and the body of Saint Francis de Sales was disinterred (it was found incorrupt), the saintly foundress received a special permission to kiss the hand of the one she loved so deeply in God. Those present witnessed, to their awe and amazement, that the hand of the holy bishop extended his arm and pressed his hand on the head of the one to whose soul he was so profoundly united.[51] This great and noble friendship has all the perfume of great human love, but it is clearly a partaking of Christ's love for the friend. For this reason, this type of relationship is based on sacrifice. What most "lovers" forget, whether

---

[51] Emile Bougaud, *St. Chantal and the Foundation of the Visitation* (New York: Benziger Brothers, 1895), 2:215.

friends or whether husband and wife, is that sacrifice is the sap of great loves.

That sacrifice is the holy vitamin of love also applies in marriage, which offers the spouses innumerable opportunities to die to themselves. There are situations in which they are clearly called upon to give up their sweet union for the sake of a higher call. If they do so, they will be rewarded by experiencing that their union has, thereby, become more sublime and a deeper source of joy.

Saint Jane's agony of sacrifice was to be duplicated in her oldest daughter, Marie-Aimée. Engaged at the age of twelve to one of the younger brothers of Saint Francis de Sales and united to him with the sweetest bonds of love, she too became a very young widow (she was nineteen and expecting their first child). Her beloved husband had been called to fulfill his military duty as a captain and had been sent to Piedmont, where, soon upon arriving, he caught a sickness that brought him to the grave. The pages dedicated to this tragedy in Monsignor Emile Bougaud's book *St. Chantal and the Foundation of the Visitation* are bound to bring tears to the reader's eyes.[52] The profound grief of Saint Francis de Sales, the heartbreak of Saint Jane, and the despair of Marie-Aimée are sketched in deeply moving words.

Marie-Aimée — like her mother before her — broke into sobs. Heroically, the young wife accepted God's

---

[52] Ibid., 2:17ff.

will and died a few months later, giving birth to a boy who died after having been baptized by his grandmother. Dedication to God, far from preventing Saint Jane from caring for her children, had deepened and purified this ardent and passionate motherly heart. Clearly, the love between Marie-Aimée and the young Baron de Thorens was a baptized love. Once the human heart is purified, its capacity to love is not only purified but deepened. A heart totally given to God, far from losing its natural tenderness, discovers that it is deepened because it is purified.

This leads us to draw two conclusions. First, the type of love to which we are alluding was inconceivable before the New Testament, as interpreted by both the Roman Catholic Church and the Orthodox Church in their devotion to Mary. Noble and great as was Jacob's love for Rachel, he who worked for some fourteen years in order to win her, it is only through Christ and with Christ that holy friendships are possible.

Second, one may also claim that the very possibility of these holy unions sheds light on the words of the Liturgy on Good Friday, *felix culpa*. The chasm that sin has created between our guilty parents has not only been spanned; more than that, through Christ, it has opened the door to a totally new dimension of union between man and woman. It has given us a golden key, a participation in Christ's love for the loved one. It is a foretaste of heaven.

CHAPTER 6
Women and the Priesthood

One of the main problems Catholic feminists have with the Church is that women are barred from the priesthood. They do not hesitate to claim that they have all the talents necessary for the sacred task and are tempted, when thinking of the mediocrity of some pastors, to assert that they would do a much better job.

Pope John Paul II made it clear that the refusal to ordain women is not based merely on a positive (or man-made) law, which could be abrogated, but is founded on a key tenet of revelation.[1] It is only in monotheistic religions that there are no goddesses or priestesses. This solemn declaration has not softened the feminists' position; it is, to their minds, once again, a form of "male imperialism." This is a huge topic, and much has been written about it. All we wish to do is to highlight some of what we

---

[1] John Paul II, Apostolic Letter *Ordinatio Sacerdotalis* (May 22, 1994), no. 4.

believe to be the most powerful arguments against this impossible demand.

HOLY DISCRIMINATION

The main arguments of feminism against the solemn proclamation of the Church that women cannot be ordained to the priesthood can be summarized by a single word: *discrimination*. Is it true that women are discriminated against when they are denied ordination?

The primary meaning of the word *discrimination* used to be "to make distinctions, to note differences." One distinguishes, for example, between the refined and the vulgar, between the intelligent and the stupid, and between the cultivated and the boorish. To have a "discriminating taste" is definitely a compliment. The prophet Isaiah writes, "Woe to those who call evil good and good evil."[2] In these words we are told that not only is such discrimination a virtue, but not to discriminate is deadly.

The sixties brought about not only political revolutions but religious, artistic, and cultural ones as well. Current usage has shifted, and a very different—predominantly negative—meaning of the word *discrimination* has emerged: "the act of looking down upon, of treating unjustly, of being unfair."

In the last fifty years, practically everyone has discovered that he has been discriminated against,

---

[2] Is 5:20.

that he has been treated unfairly because of his ethnic background, his physical appearance, the color of his skin, his weight, and so forth. This has been a field day for lawyers. Innumerable lawsuits are launched because someone believes, rightly or wrongly, that he has been "discriminated against."

That there are crying injustices cannot be challenged, but in our society, the conviction that one is being discriminated against has become epidemic. Heads of companies hesitate to fire inefficient workers because it is most likely that the one who gets a pink slip will lodge a lawsuit crying "discrimination."

One is not contesting that there are legitimate cases of unjust treatment, but the sinful human heart will always find means to pervert the law. Christ said, "There will always be poor among you."[3] He certainly does not mean to say that therefore nothing should be done to alleviate poverty. He is telling us that the evil one is the prince of the world, and as long as his head has not been crushed, injustice will prevail. Similarly, we can say, "There will always be unjust discrimination among you." Once again, it does not mean that we should not fight against injustice by every possible means, but we must understand that while we can multiply laws, *those laws cannot change the sinful human heart*. Italian common sense produced the following proverb: "Fatta la legge; trovato l'inganno" (Create

---
[3] Cf. Jn 12:8.

the law and you create the loophole). The very moment that a law is enacted, there is a way to escape from its net. Collaboration with divine grace alone can purify the world. Alas, it is a sad fact that oftentimes, when those who have been unjustly discriminated against win the upper hand, they pay back their oppressors with interest. Contrast this to the Christian teaching. Saint Paul tells us in his First Epistle to the Corinthians that we should prefer to be cheated rather than to take our brother to court.[4] Blessed are those whose ears, purified by grace, will perceive this divine message.

HOLY DISCRIMINATION VERSUS DICTATORIAL RELATIVISM

The ruling principle of the modern world is relativism. "Dictatorial relativism"[5] commands us to eliminate all hierarchical distinctions. Statements and propositions that are "true for oneself" may not be true for another person. To call some modern churches shockingly "ugly" is, under this philosophical tyranny, arrogant and undemocratic. To place Bach, Mozart, and Beethoven above rock and roll should be condemned as "elitist" and as an unfair

---

[4] 1 Cor 6:1–6.

[5] "We are building a dictatorship of relativism that does not recognize anything as definitive and whose ultimate goal consists solely of one's own ego and desires." Joseph Cardinal Ratzinger, homily at the Mass "Pro Eligendo Romano Pontifice" (April 18, 2005).

imposition of subjective taste on others. The individual subject is the "measure of all things."[6] *Truth*, *moral values*, and *beauty* are empty words. What matters is what the individual accepts as true, what he calls morally good, what *he* likes. It is all up to the individual taste. This is true "democracy." This is the philosophy that will guarantee universal harmony and peace! This is "the climate of the time."

This is an extraordinarily oppressive philosophy, whose nefarious and unhealthy chains are exposed best by the Bible. Jews and Christians acknowledge that the Bible is the word of God. This Holy Book is, however, "discriminating" from beginning to end, an action we shall call *holy discrimination*. Our first parents, Adam and Eve, were made in God's image and likeness. None of the creatures that preceded them were given this privilege. To return to Saint Bonaventure's terminology, the latter were only "traces" of God (*vestigia*).[7] Man alone was an *imago Dei* (image of God).

From the very beginning, then, God, for reasons unknown to us, placed some beings above others, and He favored some people more than others. Innumerable examples could be given. Abraham was chosen by God for no specific reason. Similarly,

---

[6] The philosopher Protagoras (c. 485–410 B.C.), the first of the Greek Sophists, is known for his dictum "Man is the measure of all things." Plato refuted this dictum in the *Theaetetus*.

[7] Bonaventure, *The Soul's Journey into God*, chap. 2, nos. 1–7.

it is written in the Holy Book: "I have loved Jacob but I have hated Esau."[8] Why are the Jewish people God's chosen ones? God does not have to justify His decisions. He never said that He chose them because they were superior. That is His decision. *Causa finita est* (The matter is settled). Pious Jews know that their being God's Chosen People is not due to their own merits. They realize that such privilege is a clarion call for them to be grateful to the Giver, to adore, serve, and obey His commands. More is required of those who have received more. It is to them that God revealed Himself. He lovingly guided them by speaking to them either directly, as He did through Moses, or by sending them prophets who were His mouthpiece and who, alas, were often murdered by their beneficiaries.

This is not the end of Scripture's clear record of "discrimination." Aaron, Moses' brother, and his tribe, that of Levi, alone were permitted to serve in the temple. This triggered the revolt of Korah, Dathan, and Abiram. They strongly objected to being forbidden to perform priestly services. After all, "all the congregation are holy," and were not all Jews equal?[9] Their punishment was eloquent: the earth opened up, and they perished with their wives and children. That was God's speedy response to their revolt.

---

[8] Mal 1:2–3.
[9] Num 16:3.

David was preceded by seven brothers. All of them were presented to Samuel, but he did not recognize in any of them the one that God wanted him to anoint. He asked their father whether he had more children. Yes, he was told, the youngest, David, who was tending the sheep. He was the one God had chosen to become king of Israel. It was God's choice. The seven brothers were "discriminated against" but, in this instance, wisely did not revolt.

These are a few among many of the divine choices that we find in the Old Testament. The "why" is not given, and recalling the words of God to Job, "Where were you when I laid the foundation of the earth? Tell me, if you have understanding,"[10] a reverent creature would not dare raise the question. He accepts God's will because it is His holy will.

In the New Testament, this "discrimination" is still more emphatic, beginning with a young virgin of Nazareth named Mary, the one who, full of grace, was asked to become the Theotokos, the Mother of the Savior, the blessed one par excellence. There were thousands of Jewish girls who longed to give birth to the Savior of Israel. Only one was chosen. To prepare her for this amazing mission, she is conceived immaculate, a unique exception to the universal curse affecting the human race since original sin. Why was Mary unaffected

---

[10] Job 38:4.

by original sin and placed above the angels, upsetting the metaphysical hierarchy that gives priority to pure spirits over human beings made up of matter and spirit? Because it was God's will.

When Christ began His public life at the age of thirty, He chose twelve apostles, those "whom he desired."[11] No explanation is given. Three among them were clearly favored: Peter, James, and John. Of these, Peter alone is chosen to be the head of the Church. Christ did not give pride of place to Saint John, "the disciple whom he loved,"[12] but to Peter, the Rock, who had denied Him three times. So was His will.

In response to man's protests that God's ways are unfair, Jesus offers us the parable of the men working in the vineyard.[13] All are paid equally, though some work from early morning and some work only at the end of the day. Those who work the whole day protest, forgetting that they received the pay they had agreed upon. The master of the vineyard, aware of their jealousy, reminds them that they had been fairly treated. Why should they object to the master's generosity and kindness toward the latecomers?

After His Resurrection, Christ became visible only to those He chose.[14] Always, we are reminded that

---

[11] Mk 3:13.

[12] Jn 19:26; cf. also Jn 13:23; 20:2; 21:7; 21:20.

[13] Mt 20:1–16.

[14] Acts 10:40–41.

He is the Lord. In the Acts of the Apostles, Saint Luke writes, "He had given commandment through the Holy Spirit to the apostles whom he had chosen."[15] On Ascension Day, when He walked for the last time through the "faithless" city, accompanied by His disciples, He was invisible "to the eyes of the people who denied Him, but visible to His disciples."[16]

As a final Scriptural example, and one that pertains specifically to the issue of the priesthood, we read in Saint Paul's Epistle to the Hebrews where he tells us that "one does not take the honor upon himself, but he is called by God, just as Aaron was."[17] These ought to be sobering words. The question is never whether or not women have the talents required for the priesthood but whether God has chosen to have women priests. The answer is clearly no.

NON SERVIAM

In his last work, *The Laws*, Plato laments the fact that man, "foolish fellow . . . is his own God."[18] He reminds us that that our weak metaphysical position should teach us some modesty and some wisdom.[19]

---

[15] Acts 1:2.

[16] Prosper Guéranger, *The Liturgical Year* (Westminster, Md.: Newman Press, 1948–1949), feast of the Ascension of Our Lord, 9:170.

[17] Heb 5:4.

[18] Plato, *The Laws*, trans. Benjamin Jowett (New York: Cosimo, 2008), no. 917, p. 262.

[19] Ibid., no. 923.

We are creatures of a day. Back in the fifties, Dietrich von Hildebrand expressed a similar thought and diagnosed a metaphysical sickness that has since become epidemic: man forgets that he is a creature.[20]

In his 2006 speech in Regensburg,[21] our Holy Father Pope Benedict XVI made it eloquently clear that philosophy (the love of wisdom) is of crucial importance in human life. Philosophy should enable us to share with people of other faiths that which can and should be shared without fear of conflict. Our bond is a common love of truth accessible to human reason. Alas, many so-called philosophers have betrayed philosophy. In *The Republic*, Plato laments the fact that bad philosophers make "blessed philosophy" very unpopular by forgetting that a philosopher should be, first and foremost, an ardent "lover of truth."[22] *Corruptio optimi pessima* (The corruption of the best is the worst of all). Starting with the Renaissance, true lovers of wisdom have been more and more replaced by what Maritain calls "ideologues," who, preferring themselves to truth, have

---

[20] Dietrich von Hildebrand, *The New Tower of Babel* (New Providence, N.J.: P. J. Kenedy and Sons, 1953), p. 14.

[21] Benedict XVI, "Faith, Reason and the University: Memories and Reflections," Aula Magna of the University of Regensburg (September 12, 2006).

[22] Cf. Plato, *The Republic*, in *The Dialogues of Plato*, trans. B. Jowett, 3rd ed., vol. 3 (Oxford: Clarendon Press, 1892), nos. 489ff., 186ff.

their own subjective agenda. The amount of harm they have done cannot be calculated.

Some of these thinkers are clearly continuing the revolt against man's creaturehood. Ludwig Feuerbach comes to mind. In his book *The Essence of Christianity*, he makes the powerful "discovery" that the being we called God is only a projection of all good and noble human qualities into an imaginary being. He says it is high time that man claims what is his lawful possession. Once this great "discovery" was put in print, it was almost inevitable that subsequent thinkers would draw the logical consequences and view God as man's enemy. Dietrich Kerler wrote that even if God's existence could be proven mathematically, he would still reject it, because it would limit his self-glory.[23] Nietzsche, pursuing the same line of thought, declared bluntly that he did not want God to exist. For such "philosophers," it is not a question of truth. It is a question of choice and taste.

The *non serviam* (I will not serve) of Lucifer is now couched in philosophical terms. Atheism is a willful choice. Man is tired of being a creature and seeing himself as weak, a metaphysical beggar, on his knees, and constantly depending upon an authoritarian master. Man has come of age. Man should now be

---

[23] Letter to Max Scheler, quoted in Henri de Lubac, *The Drama of Atheist Humanism* (San Francisco: Ignatius Press, 1995), p. 58.

in command. The mind-boggling scientific and technological advances of the last sixty years seem, to certain susceptible personalities, to validate this arrogant claim.

The whole question hinges on whether or not man is a creature. Whether we like it or not, we are mortal. There is nothing like facing death to make us realize our weakness and vulnerability. To deny our creaturehood does not make us gods. It just proves our stupidity. This attitude of revolt gives us a key to the "drama of atheist humanism" that is the cancer of our society.

How right Kierkegaard was when he focused on the concept of defiance as the root of metaphysical doubt. He explained his own "aberrations" of faith as expressions of revolt against his father, and therefore against God. It is his claim that rebellion against Christianity is first and foremost an act of defiance, under the pretext of intellectual doubt. The latter is a cover-up. It is therefore useless to wage an intellectual war on "doubt" when in fact the battle should be on an ethical ground against rebellion.[24] Kierkegaard's claim that rebellion is the *only* key to atheism remains an open question. But (anticipating Nietzsche) his claim that revolt and defiance clearly play a role in some cases cannot be

---

[24] Søren Kierkegaard, *Journals* (1847), quoted in Walter Lowrie, *Kierkegaard*, vol. 1 (New York: Oxford University Press, 1938), p. 187.

denied. There are certain truths that are unpalatable to human pride.

THE OBEDIENCE OF THE CREATURE

The intelligent attitude of someone who realizes that he is "but a creature" is to listen and obey. Once again, the Bible gives us examples of religious men who became heroes of faith. When Abraham was told to leave his country, he did so without questioning God. When Moses was ordered to go to Pharaoh and tell him to let the enslaved Jewish people leave Egypt, he dared raise an objection: to select someone suffering from a speech defect did not seem to him a wise choice. God became irate: "The anger of the LORD was kindled against Moses."[25] But Moses did go, accompanied by his brother to speak for him. God always chooses weak instruments to achieve His purpose.

Man's response to a divine order, no matter how baffling that order may sound, should be obedience. The weaker we are, the greater should be our trust that God, and God alone, will achieve victory. When the young Samuel heard a voice calling him by name, he got up immediately, assuming that Eli had called him. He was told that such was not the case. The same scenario was repeated two more times, after which Eli told the young boy that it was God calling

---

[25] Ex 4:14.

him. When the voice was heard again, the young boy said only, "Speak, for your servant hears."[26]

In another Scripture passage, when the deacon Philip, on his way to Gaza, was told to join a pagan in a chariot, he obeyed and brought a soul to God.[27] This is the attitude adopted by all saints. This willingness to listen to God's voice is a habit abandoned by "modern man," who, believing that he has come of age, asserts that it is now his right to claim his independence. In Pergolese's opera *La serva padrona*, the composer presents the ludicrous case of a servant who gives commands to her master. This is pretty much what is happening today. Instead of saying with Samuel, "Speak, O Lord, for your servant hears," modern man now says, "Hear, O God, for your servant commands." This attitude can be traced back to a total loss of the sense of the supernatural, that is, of faith.

Man, inebriated by his mind-boggling technological advances (more radical changes have taken place in the course of the last sixty years than in the whole history of humanity), has convinced himself that he can now conquer the universe, aging, and death. God was a crutch that is no longer needed. Man is now God. We are promised that in a not too distant future, we shall have perfect control over our destiny. It is worth remarking that men are ever more

---

[26] 1 Sam 3:10.

[27] Acts 8:26–40.

concerned about prolonging lives that have become more and more meaningless. Suffering, we are told, will be under control. In fact, it is not suffering that is unbearable—it is meaningless suffering. Despair is the proper response to meaningless suffering. This is the modern sickness par excellence as diagnosed by Kierkegaard in *Sickness unto Death*.

It is one thing for man to dream that he is God, and quite another to convince himself that this discovery has brought peace and joy on earth. The twentieth century will probably go down in history as the bloodiest, cruelest, most brutal of all centuries. Gabriel Marcel wrote, "God is dead. Man is agonizing."[28] We have reasons to fear that he is right. There is little chance that the twenty-first century will be any better unless there is an extraordinary conversion of hearts.

It is important to recognize that once God's primacy as King is challenged and denied, man's perception of the hierarchical structure of the universe is shaken. If man is on a level with God, the distinction between the morally good and the morally evil, the distinction between beauty and ugliness, the distinction between true and false, the distinction between refinement and vulgarity also topple. This is not accidental. Everything stands or falls according to whether or not God's divine Kingship is recognized.

---

[28] "Dieu est mort, l'homme est en agonie." Gabriel Marcel, *Les hommes contre l'humain* (Paris: La Colombe, 1951), p. 18.

To relegate Him—and therefore the reality He has established—to the domain of myth is to call down disaster on humanity. We have entered apocalyptic times: *Jerusalem, Jerusalem, convertere ad Dominum tuum* (Jerusalem, Jerusalem, return to your God).[29]

DEFIANCE MASQUERADING AS DOUBT

Once a person has adopted a basic attitude of defiance, all sorts of questions are bound to arise that never enter a human mind as long as man is in the right "metaphysical posture." When God ordered Adam and Eve not to eat of the fruit of one particular tree in the earthly paradise, they did not question His order. To bring our first parents to disobey, the evil one used a very simple technique. He raised a question that had not crossed their minds: *Why not?* To modern man, that question seems to be something innocuous. Is man, as a rational being, not entitled to ask questions? One clear fact, however, has been almost entirely obscured and forgotten: *there are questions that are raised only when man has adopted a wrong metaphysical posture*. Once he has lost his sense that he is a creature, and that reality is ordered by God and not by the creature's whim, then his outlook becomes lopsided and his mind twisted and dysfunctional. This wrong metaphysical posture (which Dietrich von Hildebrand calls a rejection of man's metaphysical

---

[29] Office of Holy Saturday, Matins, First Nocturn.

situation)[30] gives us a master key to innumerable aberrations—theological, metaphysical, epistemological, and ethical—that have spread like a plague through the centuries. All of a sudden, the feeble human mind, darkened by sin, started raising innumerable questions that a person in the right posture would not dream of raising: Why are certain acts condemned as immoral? Why should anyone tell us what we should do and not do? He begins to ask: Why should one not be a sadist if it gives one pleasure? Why should one be prohibited from abusing babies? Why should man be placed above animals? Why should certain pleasurable actions be called perversions? The list is literally endless.

Such questions do not call for an answer. They should be rejected with horror. They do not stem from any genuine desire to know; instead, they attempt to impose one's passions and wishes upon reality. This masquerade hides the root assumption that there is neither God nor devil, and therefore no good or evil. This assumption is a first principle, not an intellectual argument. It is a willed blindness to the great facts of being, beauty, truth, goodness, and order. If a person is color-blind, he should trust those whose eyesight is normal and not argue about colors. It is crucial that a sick person should realize that the problem is in him. It is only by healing that he comes to relearn what health feels like.

---

[30] Von Hildebrand, *New Tower of Babel*, p. 10.

THE DISTORTED QUESTION OF FEMININE PRIESTHOOD: NO ENTITLEMENT

Up to now, we have spoken about what we called "holy discriminations." God is King. It is up to Him to decide what He wants to do. Therefore, it is arrogant to claim that women are *entitled* to be ordained priests.

There are those who claim, however, that if the Catholic Church proclaims, "No, women are not entitled to be ordained priests," this simply proves that the Church views women as second-class citizens. They wonder aloud how, under such circumstances, half of the human race can feel "at home" in an organization dominated by the male sex. They call it a "male church."

To place the question in proper perspective, we should recall that through original sin, we lost the unmerited gift of supernatural life. Moreover, our intelligence was darkened, our will weakened, and our heart hardened. Through the loving condescension of the God-man Who assumed our human nature, not only has supernatural life been restored to us, but we have been offered a lesson in humility. The sin of our first parents was primarily a sin of pride; the redemptive action of the God-man was an infinite gesture of humility.

That God chose to become man is truly a sign of divine madness. Humility is the cure offered to sinful man, but this virtue, learned and practiced through the acceptance of humiliations, is so distasteful to man's fallen nature that to him it is worse than death. There is nothing man loathes more than to be humiliated; he dreads it even more than suffering. Indeed, many people would prefer physical torture to being publicly humiliated. Our fallen nature remains allergic to the cure our Savior has brought us.

It is typical of pride to revolt, to dissent, to refuse to bend its neck, and to disobey a legitimate authority. The Old Testament records the story of a people in constant rebellion because they resented the burdens of the Law that their divine election put upon their shoulders. One would expect that, since Christians have a new Covenant that is a covenant of love, this rebellious tendency would be tamed. That is far from being the case. Christians also rebel against the sweet burden of the supernatural. We are like the Gadarenes who begged Christ to leave their territory after they had witnessed the miraculous healing of a man with an unclean spirit.[31] One would expect them to thank the Savior and to beg Him to remain with them. Instead, they asked Him to depart. The supernatural had come uncomfortably close to them. How right Kierkegaard was when he wrote that we are all, more or less, afraid of the truth.[32] One of the

---

[31] Mt 8:28–34.
[32] Søren Kierkegaard, *The Journals of Kierkegaard*, trans. Alexander Dru (New York: Harper Torch Books, 1959), p. 202.

saddest sayings in Saint Paul's Epistles is the one he addresses to the Galatians: "Have I then become your enemy by telling you the truth?"[33] Christ would not have been crucified had He not brought the Truth that He Himself was to sinful humanity.

Women who know the Church with the eyes of faith, thanks to God's grace, would never dream of raising the question, "Why can't we be ordained?" As soon as we cease to believe that God is behind nature, it sounds perfectly rational and legitimate to ask why different missions are assigned to men and women. Some bishops are very mediocre; there have been very bad popes. Women, given the chance, could do no worse, and some of them are deeply convinced they could do much better. "After all," they truly quote the Church, "all human beings have equal dignity." They may go on, "Does not Saint Paul write that from now on 'there is neither male nor female; for you are all one in Christ Jesus'?"[34] Quoting some truths of the faith itself, feminist rhetoric proceeds to ask why men should be placed above women. Why should a purely biological difference be a valid reason for excluding half of humanity from a supernatural privilege granted to the male sex? Why should women, usually more intuitive than men and endowed with a greater degree of empathy, be judged incapable of

---

[33] Gal 4:16.
[34] Gal 3:28.

hearing confessions and giving absolution? Is not this an arbitrary and unfair law? Finally, they insinuate that with even a minimal knowledge of sociology we can judge that "Christ Himself did not ordain women only because He was still bound by the customs of His time."

All of this sounds very convincing to ears not attuned to the supernatural, and alas, modern man has developed a severe deafness to its music. The supernatural is the warp and woof of Christianity: Christianity stands or falls with it. Given the *Zeitgeist* (the spirit of the time), which emphasizes man's "maturity" and his craving for independence, it is hard indeed to accept a teaching soaked in humility. To modern sensibilities, to obey is to be craven or to deny man's dignity. Man is entitled to take his life into his own hands and to make his own decisions.

To be told that we should love our enemies, to forgive those who have offended us (even though they show no sign of repentance), to offer the left cheek when struck on the right one,[35] is a difficult instruction. That we should give our tunic to the person who already has taken our cloak, to be told that we should prefer to be defrauded than to take our brother to court[36] — these are commands that not only challenge elementary common sense but

---

[35] Mt 5:44.
[36] Mt 5:40; 1 Cor 6:7.

sound discordant to the modern ear. Modern man, however, is no more entitled to be an enemy of the Cross than his forebears were. His much-desired "self-fulfillment" and earthly happiness, ironically, are all the more elusive, for he violates the very laws that might provide them.

Blind to the supernatural message, feminists claim that the Christian message should be reinterpreted in the light of modern scholarship, modern psychology, and modern biblical criticism. Our knowledge—so unsatisfactory and fragmentary in the past—should now be updated to prove the claim that women have been "kept down" by the dominant male sex. The problem is that they read the divine message with secularist lenses. They forget that, to quote Kierkegaard, the Bible should be read "on one's knees," with an attitude of humble receptivity. Otherwise, he says, inevitably "wine will be changed into water."[37] When supernatural being is silently denied and divine "discrimination" loudly condemned as unfair and undemocratic, the feminists' claim that they are entitled to be ordained rings loudly in the emptied air.

Within this antisupernatural stance, superficial characteristics are substituted for the deeper, essen-

---

[37] "For our age does not stop with faith, with its miracle of turning water into wine; it goes further, it turns wine into water." Søren Kierkegaard, *Fear and Trembling*, trans. Alastair Hannay (London: Penguin Classics, 1985), p. 67.

tial character of men and women. It makes perverse sense to praise Saint Paul, not as an apostle and martyr, but as a "genius," comparable to Einstein. In one television program, a man declared Blessed Teresa of Calcutta and Ted Turner to be his two icons. For him they were equally admirable persons; he most admired them because both of them started from scratch and achieved amazing results. In such a "vision" the Holy Virgin is praised for her stamina and resiliency, standing at the foot of the Cross. The bishop of Chur, Switzerland—handpicked by the pope—was rejected by his sheep for not having a Ph.D. The people's choice had the title "Doctor" in front of his name. These instances, which could be multiplied ad nauseam, demonstrate the contemporary tendency to eschew the profound and meaningful for surface characteristics.

How readily we forget that God chooses what is weak.[38] Did God make an unwise choice in sending a man who suffered from a speech defect to Pharaoh? Any intelligent man would have chosen Demosthenes or Cicero. How could Christ choose uncultivated and "primitive" men to be His apostles? Human wisdom would have sought out the well-trained and learned rabbis in Palestine; they seemed much better equipped to spread His message. Peter denied Christ three times. Why was he chosen to be the first pope when human wisdom can see that

---

[38] 1 Cor 1:27.

John, the one disciple at the foot of the Cross, would have been a better candidate? Once again, we are facing the abyss separating supernature from nature. "Learned men," being learned, usually refuse to admit that their earthly wisdom is foolishness. Saint Paul is explicit on the question, and he glories exclusively in his weakness.[39] God's work is accomplished not by efficiency and talents but by holiness, and there is no holiness without a joyful acknowledgment that without God we can do nothing.[40] He who has fulfilled the task assigned to him is and remains no more than an "unworthy" servant.[41]

Christ said, "Blessed is he who takes no offense at me."[42] Contemporary feeling, however, finds it "offensive" to transcend a purely natural outlook and endorse a supernatural one. Like the Cross, Christ remains a scandal for the Jews and foolishness to the Gentiles.[43] However, the supernatural fact remains: women are not called by Christ to be priests in His Church. Only those who fully accept God's will are in the right posture to penetrate divine mysteries. Feminists, by rejecting God's will on the priesthood, disqualify themselves from their own desire. In this light, one thing should be clear: the feminists claiming their rights to the priesthood scorn the supernat-

---

[39] 2 Cor 11:30.
[40] Jn 15:5.
[41] Lk 17:10.
[42] Mt 11:6.
[43] 1 Cor 1:23.

ural will of God—as did Korah, Dathan, and Abiram in their revolt against Moses and Aaron because they were not permitted to become priests. God gave the final answer, and it was fearful.

MATERNITY AND THE PRIESTHOOD

From a standpoint of obedience to God's will, it is clear. Maternity and priesthood are two complementary but incompatible charismas. ***They are jeweled crosses, too heavy to be carried simultaneously***.

We have tried to shed some modest light on the greatness of maternity, which is the charisma par excellence confided to women. To be "the mother of life" is an aristocratic title of such greatness and beauty that it was bound to be the main target of the evil one's attacks. This awesome privilege is linked to deep sufferings, not only from childbearing and childbirth, but from the constant yearning to help form the beloved fruit of her womb to his eternal destiny: his union with God. We need only speak to a "real mother" to realize that, as long as she lives, she continues to "give birth." How she trembles when her child is sick, when he suffers, when she realizes that she cannot protect him from harm or that he will be exposed to grave temptations that might endanger his eternal salvation. When he makes decisions that are clearly going to harm him and those around him, she is devastated. Saint Monica comes to mind. The pains she endured giving physical birth to Augustine were mild compared to the anguish she experienced when he was living in sin.

The young virgin who sang the Magnificat — "The Lord has done great things for me" — is also the *mater dolorosa*. To be a mother is to carry a bejewelled cross, intrinsically linked to suffering. It is a sweet but heavy burden.[44]

The same can be said about the priesthood. It is an unfathomable honor given to some men, an honor called by Dom Guéranger "the dread honour of the Priesthood."[45] Saint Francis of Assisi, that wonderfully holy man, felt unworthy of such "dread honor." Similarly, it is related in the life of the holy Curé d'Ars that when he carried the sacred Host in procession, his face was covered with sweat. He was so conscious of carrying the Living God that it was experienced as a weight that only grace enabled him to carry. Guéranger's words express that priests truly worthy of the priesthood perceive such a discrepancy between the honor bestowed upon them and their human frailty that, if not sustained by the grace of the sacrament, the task would be beyond their human strength.

How humbling for a pope to be called "Your Holiness." He fully knows his frailty; he fully knows himself to be in need of redemption. Yet he

---

[44] In this context, we refrain to speak of the greatness of fatherhood, only because our subject is women and the priesthood.

[45] Guéranger, *Liturgical Year*, Ember Days of September, 11:393.

is the representative of the Savior of the world. Jacques Maritain suggested that such titles should now be abolished, as if they no longer are appropriate for our time. My objection is that such a change would deprive the successors of Saint Peter of *the healthy daily humiliation of receiving in their persons a homage properly given only to the One they represent.* To my mind, it is a superb form of penance, daily highlighting the prayer: "Not to us, O LORD, not to us, but to your name give glory."[46]

As is the case with maternity, the priesthood fully lived is a life of crucifixion. It cannot be repeated often enough that on this earth, the deepest joys and the most excruciating sorrows are so closely linked to each other that they cannot be separated. As soon as we realize that a priest is to be an *alter Christus* (another Christ)—that he is given the power to change bread and wine into the body and blood of the Lord or that he can say to a repentant sinner, "Go in peace; your sins are forgiven"—we must marvel at the fact that some people dare claim that they are *entitled* to this dignity. The classical Catholic words, "Lord, I am not worthy," are replaced by, "Of course I am worthy. I *feel* that I am."

MATERNAL ASPIRATIONS

The deepest wish of many holy mothers is that their sons will be called to the priesthood. When he is

---
[46] Ps 115:1.

ordained, her motherly heart will be overcome by a "holy pride." She feels unworthy to have given birth to someone who represents Christ and who has been granted the power to pronounce the sacred words, in *persona Christi*, "This is my body; this is my blood."

Alas, there are cases when mothers, tempted by a very subtle vanity, keep *telling* their sons that it is their greatest wish. Desirous to fulfill their mother's most ardent desire, there are young men who enter the priesthood without having received this noble vocation. Not surprisingly, they are unhappy and ill-suited to the task. A selfless mother should confide her wish to God and practice holy discretion, from fear of exercising an illegitimate influence upon her child. True love is selfless love.

How selfless was the attitude of Saint Monica. She prayed ardently that her son might live in God's grace. Marriage seemed to be the solution. But God gave her much more than what she had requested. Augustine decided to give his whole life to God. "She saw that through me you had given her far more that she had long begged for by her piteous tears and groans."[47]

A saintly woman, Margarita, the mother of Saint John Bosco, while helping him in every way to attain his dream, the priesthood, never put any pressure on

---

[47] *The Confessions of St. Augustine*, trans. John K. Ryan (New York: Doubleday, 1960), bk. 8, no. 30, p. 203.

him. She was an illiterate peasant woman, but she had a truly Christian heart and, with unfailing wisdom and patience, guided her son toward God. The very day that John was ordained, she said to him, "Be sure to remember this: *beginning to say Mass means beginning to suffer*."[48] If maternity is a sweet but heavy burden, so is the priesthood. As mentioned above, these two bejeweled crosses cannot be carried simultaneously; they would be too heavy.

To be priest also means to be victim; this is what I mean by "bejeweled cross." This is what Mamma Margarita intimated to her son on the day of his ordination. A mother brings life into the world. A priest — a victim — sacrifices his life to bring souls to God.

MODEST APPEARANCE

According to the divine plan, then, women have a crucial role to play in the economy of redemption. The moment they revolt against the mission God has chosen for them, the consequences are tragic. Marriage, the family, society at large, and Holy Church are all affected by this "defection." He who wishes to kill a person aims at his heart. This is why Josef Cardinal Ratzinger wrote, as cited in chapter 2, that the feminist revolution is of such gravity.

According to whether or not women live up to their noble calling, men will respond to them with

---

[48] A. Auffray, *Blessed John Bosco (1815–1888)*, trans. W. H. Mitchell (New York: Benzinger Brothers, 1930), p. 60.

either respect or contempt. They know that women can kindle what is best in them (chivalrous feelings) or what is worst in them (unbridled lust) and will act in accord with the sometimes very subtle "message" that a woman sends them. For this reason, Saint Paul admonishes women to "adorn themselves modestly,"[49] telling them that the secret that is in them must be protected by the veil of holy *pudeur* (modesty).

How deplorable that, misreading the message of Vatican II, so many nuns no longer wear their habits and veils. Universal tradition tells us that the way people are attired communicates a message about their person and their dignity. Kings wear a crown; popes wear the tiara. Each religious order had its own habit that distinguished it from other religious orders. Nowadays, however, it is impossible to distinguish some nuns from career women, let alone a Franciscan from a Sister of Charity. The symbolic meaning of clothes is so deeply imprinted on the human soul that the Franciscan Friars of the Renewal—a contemporary male order that has returned to wearing a full habit—will tell you that the very sight of their cowl and habit always triggers a response of respect on the part of the public. One of them marveled that even prostitutes treat him with great reverence. The monks' very appearance sends a message. In the Tridentine Liturgy,

---

[49] 1 Tim 2:9.

the celebrant has to don seven pieces of clothing, each one of them symbolic of one facet of Christ's ascension to Golgotha. Josef Cardinal Ratzinger wrote in his great book on the Liturgy that "bending the knee before the presence of the living God is something we cannot abandon."[50] This book is a gem, constantly reminding us of the symbolic meaning of actions and vestments. Bodily posture has always carried a message. Let us recall the importance that Saint Benedict grants to it in his rule. He knew that a reverent bodily posture helps recollection and that recollection calls for a corresponding body language.[51]

A VOCATION OF OBEDIENCE

Feminists repeatedly say that women will no longer tolerate to be treated as second-class citizens. Apparently, many of the bishops are impressed by the feminist plea to be granted a place in the Church, where they feel alienated. For the sake of argument, let us assume that women have, in fact, been unfairly treated in the Catholic Church. One possible response—the one of feminists—is bitterness and revolt, leading progressively to a total rejection of the Christian message. Another is to meditate on the words of Isaiah and contemplate

---

[50] Joseph Cardinal Ratzinger, *The Spirit of the Liturgy* (San Francisco: Ignatius Press, 2000), p. 191.

[51] *Rule of Saint Benedict*, 9.

the life and death of our Savior.[52] He was ridiculed, slapped, spit upon, tortured, and crucified. It is understandable when someone rejects Christianity because he refuses to carry the Cross and follow the Holy One to Golgotha. But what is not understandable is to insist upon calling oneself Christian while systematically rejecting the very core of Christianity, the imitation of Christ.

In her autobiography, as previously cited, Saint Thérèse of Lisieux writes that when traveling in Italy, she was constantly told not to go here or there because women were prohibited from entering under the penalty of excommunication. Commenting upon this, she proceeds to tell us that while her sex is often held in contempt, "women had more courage than the apostles since they braved the insults of the soldiers and dared to dry the adorable Face of Jesus. It is undoubtedly because of this that He allows misunderstanding to be their lot on earth, since He chose it for Himself. In heaven, He will show that His thoughts are not men's thoughts, for then the *last will be first*."[53]

---

[52] "He was despised and rejected by men; a man of sorrows, and acquainted with grief; and as one from whom men hide their faces. . . . He was oppressed, and he was afflicted, yet he opened not his mouth" (Is 53:3, 7).

[53] Thérèse of Lisieux, *Story of a Soul: The Autobiography of Saint Thérèse of Lisieux*, trans. John Clarke, 3rd ed. (Washington, D.C.: ICS Publications, 1996), manuscript A, fol. 66v, p. 140.

Proof of one injustice is not a call for another injustice. That is not how the world is set right.

One takes the fact that many more men than women are canonized. If one were to imagine this is a convincing proof of the superiority of the male sex, he would be deceived. First of all, although to be canonized is a "proof" of holiness, not to be officially canonized does not prove that one is not a saint. There are innumerable *uncanonized* saints. For example, the Carthusians, belonging to the most perfect order in the Catholic Church, never promote the cause of their members. Only their founder, Saint Bruno, was canonized. They do not care for the recognition of men. They are so totally God-centered that any honor—even coming from the highest authority in the Church—is not on their spiritual screen. In eternity, however, we shall experience some amazing surprises and find out that millions of unknown men and women who served God with love and humility were among the just. This is the powerful message that Solzhenitsyn communicated, as clearly as he dared in a Communist state, when he wrote *Matryona's House*, the story of a poor, humble, deeply Christian peasant woman. "She never cared for smart clothes, the garments that embellish the ugly and disguise the wicked."[54] In heaven, we shall meet innumerable

---

[54] Alexander Solzhenitsyn, *Stories and Prose Poems* (London: The Bodley Head, 1971), 54, quoted in Joseph Pearce,

Matryonas who, on this earth, were looked down upon as not worthy of one's attention.

In the second place, the work of men is usually more center stage, and for this reason, it is easier to find promoters of their cause. Women used to understand intuitively that it is a privilege to follow Christ without any recognition. He who serves and suffers as an expression of love for Him will experience a joy that the world cannot give. Not to hear the expression "Thank you" grieves such faithful servants only because ingratitude offends God and stains the soul of the ungrateful one. But for all that, never will their service be done for an earthly reward, not even for a "Thank you."

ARGUMENTS FALL ON DEAF EARS

In the course of giving talks for the last twenty years, I have noticed that the classic arguments against the ordination of women mostly fall on rocky ground. They are not only rejected but usually increase the feminists' opposition. Told that it was God's will to grant the privilege of the priesthood exclusively to men, they accuse God Himself of sexism. If they are reminded that Jesus did not call His holy Mother to be ordained, they will tell you that God was still imprisoned in the sociological categories prevalent in the Jewish society at the time.

Solzhenitsyn: A Soul in Exile (Grand Rapids, Mich.: Baker Books, 2001), p. 145.

Blessed Teresa of Calcutta once said that there was only one person *entitled* to say, "This is my body; this is my blood." That was the Holy Virgin. Yet she was not called to the priesthood.[55] The sacred relationship between Mary and her divine Son gives us probably the most profound argument against the priesthood of women. A reading of the Old Testament in the light of the New (and it is the New that gives us the key to a full understanding of the Old) makes it clear that there is only *one* Priest, the Son of the Living God, Christ. The priesthood in the Old Testament is a figure of this new Priesthood. At the very moment of the Incarnation, Mary, in conceiving the second Person of the Holy Trinity made man, conceived the one Priest whose Priesthood would be consummated on Golgotha by sacrificing Himself for our salvation. Mary is therefore the Mother of the one Priest, and as it is not possible to be mother and son simultaneously, ***the Mother of the Priest cannot herself be a priest***. To such arguments the feminists respond only that the Bible is built on myths.

---

[55] "No one could have been a better priest than the Virgin Mother of God, because she really could without difficulty say: 'This is my body . . . This is my blood'—for it was really and truly her body and blood that she gave to Jesus. And yet she remained only the handmaid of the Lord, so that you and I may always turn to her as our Mother." Teresa of Calcutta, "Priestly Celibacy: Sign of the Charity of Christ," January 1, 1993, www.vatican.va/roman_curia/congregations/cclergy/documents/rc_con_cclergy_doc_01011993_sign_en.html.

If one uses a theological argument, namely, that in every sacrament there are two essential components, the matter and the form, and that the matter of the sacrament of ordination is the male sex, they will proclaim that the Church is sexist and biased.

In the light of such obstinacy, what are we going to say to women who tell us that they are deeply convinced that they have a calling to the priesthood? They sound so sincere, so deeply convinced. But however ardent a wish can be, humility teaches us that it is to be tested. All of us, and women particularly, can confuse subjective desires with an objective calling. Valuable as intellectual arguments are, the problem we are dealing with is not primarily intellectual. It is moral. The most convincing argument will never convince someone who refuses to be convinced. As I once said to a student informing me that I had not succeeded in convincing him, "I never tried to convince you. I only tried to be convincing. Now it is up to you." This is why spiritual guidance under the light of tradition should be our guide.

Mary did not *choose* to be the Mother of the Savior; she was offered the privilege. The apostles did not choose to be apostles; they were chosen. Women, to whom are confided the mystery of life, are essentially called upon to be mothers, whether they are "sterile" or whether they have been blessed with children of their own flesh. Many women have received the privilege to be the mothers of priests. Paul Evdokimov put it well: mothers are called upon to help engender Christ in their children's souls, for it is often the mother who, by her suffering and love, leads her son to the priesthood. Saints are those who discover and accept that what God chooses for us is the way to holiness. It is very often very different from what we have wished for, planned, or anticipated, but in hindsight, we shall have to acknowledge that if His ways are not our ways, that means they are the only good way.

SAINT THÉRÈSE OF LISIEUX AND THE PRIESTHOOD

The Little Flower writes that carried by the intensity of her love for Christ, she felt that to be His spouse, to be a Carmelite, to be a mother of souls, did not satisfy her longing. She wished to fulfill all possible roles and to be a warrior for Christ—a priest, an apostle, a doctor, and a martyr. Her song reaches its climax in her desire to be a martyr and shed her blood for the Beloved. Realizing the impossibility of unifying all these callings, she tells us that she suffers tortures. She cannot possibly live up to her longing. Then she turns to the First Epistle of Saint Paul to the Corinthians and understands that her vocation is love.[56] Love and love

---

[56] "So faith, hope, and love abide, these three; but the greatest of these is love" (1 Cor 13:13).

alone combines all the various callings and vocations that she ardently desired to unite.

She writes:

> It should be enough for me, Jesus, to be Your spouse, to be a Carmelite and, by union with You, to be the mother of souls. Yet I long for other vocations: I want to be a warrior, a priest, an apostle, a doctor of the Church, a martyr.... I would like to perform the most heroic deeds. I feel I have the courage of a Crusader. I should like to die on the battlefield in defence of the Church.
>
> If only I were a priest! How lovingly, Jesus, would I hold You in my hands when my words had brought You down from heaven and how lovingly would I give You to the faithful. Yet though I long to be a priest, I admire and envy the humility of St. Francis of Assisi and feel that I should imitate him and refuse the sublime dignity of the priesthood. How can I reconcile these desires?
>
> ... I should like to wander through the world, preaching Your Name and raising Your glorious Cross in pagan lands. But it would not be enough to have only one field of mission work. I should not be satisfied unless I preached the Gospel in every quarter of the globe and even in the most remote islands. Nor should I be content to be a missionary for only a few years. I should like to have been one from the creation of the world and to continue as one till the end of time. But, above all, I long to be a martyr. From my childhood I have dreamt of martyrdom, and it is a dream which has grown more and more real in my little cell in Carmel. But I don't want to suffer just one torment. I should have to suffer them all to be satisfied....

I opened the epistles of St. Paul to try to find some cure for my sufferings. And in chapter twelve and thirteen of the First Epistle to the Corinthians I read that we cannot all be apostles, prophets, and doctors, that the Church is made up of different members, and that the eye cannot also be the hand. The answer was clear enough, but it did not satisfy me and brought me no peace. But as St. John of the Cross says, "descending into the depths of my own nothingness, I was raised so high that I reached my goal." I went on reading and came to: "Be zealous for the better gifts. And I show unto you a yet more excellent way." The apostle explains how even all the most perfect gifts are nothing without love and that charity is the most excellent way of going safely to God. I had found peace at last. . . .

Swept by an ecstatic joy, I cried: "Jesus, my love! *At last I have found my vocation. My vocation is love! I have found my place in the bosom of the Church and it is You, Lord, who has given it me.*"[57]

It could not possibly be said any better than that, so we will allow the Little Flower to have the last words.

---

[57] Letter to Sister Marie of the Sacred Heart (September 8, 1896), in *The Autobiography of St. Thérèse of Lisieux: The Story of a Soul*, trans. John Beevers (New York: Image Books, 1957), manuscript B, fol. 2v, pp. 153–55.